Maths Revolution

How to turn resistance into
GCSE success

Julia Smith

BLOOMSBURY EDUCATION
LONDON OXFORD NEW YORK NEW DELHI SYDNEY

BLOOMSBURY EDUCATION
Bloomsbury Publishing Plc

Bloomsbury Publishing Plc
50 Bedford Square, London WC1B 3DP, UK

Bloomsbury Publishing Ireland Limited
29 Earlsfort Terrace, Dublin 2, D02 AY28, Ireland

BLOOMSBURY, BLOOMSBURY EDUCATION and the Diana logo are trademarks of Bloomsbury Publishing Plc

First published in Great Britain in 2026 by Bloomsbury Publishing Plc
This edition published in Great Britain in 2026 by Bloomsbury Publishing Plc

Text copyright © Julia Smith, 2026
Photographs copyright © Julia Smith, 2026, except for: Shutterstock/Raphael Ruz – *Spiral of seeds in a sunflower* (p.113); Shutterstock/Gergitek – *Tesselating tiles* (p.113); Shutterstock/SkillUp – *Optical illusion* (p.114); Shutterstock/Kenishirotie – *Geometry set* (p.123); Shutterstock/Becris – *Scientific calculator* (p.123); Shutterstock/xpixel – *Ruler* (p.126); Shutterstock/Anton Starikov – *Half-protractor* (p.127); Shutterstock/Adrenaline studio – *Full-protractor* (p.127); Shutterstock/Yevheniia BH – *Key parts of a circle* (p.130).
Julia Smith has asserted her right under the Copyright, Designs and Patents Act, 1988, to be identified as the Author of this work

Bloomsbury Publishing Plc does not have any control over, or responsibility for, any third-party websites referred to or in this book. All internet addresses given in this book were correct at the time of going to press. The author and publisher regret any inconvenience caused if addresses have changed or sites have ceased to exist, but can accept no responsibility for any such changes

All rights reserved. No part of this publication may be: i) reproduced or transmitted in any form, electronic or mechanical, including photocopying, recording or by means of any information storage or retrieval system without prior permission in writing from the publishers; or ii) used or reproduced in any way for the training, development or operation of artificial intelligence (AI) technologies, including generative AI technologies. The rights holders expressly reserve this publication from the text and data mining exception as per Article 4(3) of the Digital Single Market Directive (EU) 2019/790

A catalogue record for this book is available from the British Library

ISBN: PB: 978-1-80199-822-2; ePub: 978-1-80199-820-8
2 4 6 8 10 9 7 5 3 1

Cover design by James Fraser

Typeset by Lumina Datamatics Ltd
Printed and bound in Great Britain by TJ Books, Padstow, Cornwall

To find out more about our authors and books visit www.bloomsbury.com
and sign up for our newsletters
For product safety related questions contact productsafety@bloomsbury.com

Contents

Introduction iv

Part One Understanding Resistance 1

1 'I Hate Maths!': What's Your Answer? 3
2 Maths is Good for You! 17
3 Motivation: Moving People to Action 29

Part Two Building Foundations 41

4 Mathematical Fluency and Core Skills 43
5 Fundamental Maths Knowledge 59
6 Mathematical Methods 73

Part Three Creating Connections 93

7 Vocational and Real-life Relevance 95
8 Mathematical Hooks 115
9 Tools in the Toolbox 129

Part Four Achieving Success 145

10 Solving the Problem with Problem Solving 147
11 From Exam Panic to Exam Power 157
12 Re-vision: Seeing Maths Differently 173

Conclusion: Changing the Narrative 189
References 191
Further Reading and Resources 198
Index 199

Introduction: from mathematical resistance to resilience

A polarised view of maths

Maths is like Marmite®: you either love it or hate it, with not much in between! When I tell people what I do for a living, they respond with either admiration or horror. Being good at maths is held in high esteem, but many people are quick to suggest that it's not for them.

This divide didn't happen by itself. It's been shaped by years of classroom experiences, societal attitudes and well-meaning but ineffective teaching methods. Over two decades of working with students who struggle with maths across Key Stage 4, further education (FE) and adult learning, I've seen how this resistance builds but, more importantly, I've seen how it can be turned around, hence the title *Maths Revolution*.

When a student says 'I hate maths', it's rarely about the subject itself. It reflects repeated frustration, anxiety and not being able to see how maths fits into their life. That resistance isn't fixed; it's a learned response and, with the right support, it can be unlearned. This book is about helping you make that transformation happen. I'll give you the tools and confidence to support resistant learners in shifting their attitudes, effectively, one student at a time.

The transformation

Resistance to maths doesn't appear overnight and it won't disappear that quickly either. It's usually built up from a series of negative experiences: being embarrassed during mental arithmetic, being told they're 'not a maths person', or trying hard yet repeatedly struggling to reach Grade 4. Each experience adds more resistance. Resistance serves a purpose: it protects students from further hurt. For people who've faced repeated disappointment, avoiding these situations feels like a smart survival tactic. Your challenge is to provide new experiences that are so positive and empowering that students are willing to give maths another try.

Teaching maths is both emotional and cognitive. It involves understanding the anxiety, frustration and even shame that comes with mathematical challenges and addressing those barriers while teaching the content itself. That's why this book takes a whole-person approach: practical, inclusive and emotionally aware.

Whether you're teaching GCSE resit students, supporting hesitant learners in Years 10 and 11, or working with adults returning to education, you'll find strategies here that work in real classrooms, not just in theory.

Your mathematical toolbox

Throughout this book we'll build a multi-layered mathematical toolbox. Each layer serves a specific purpose, from laying solid foundations to developing advanced problem-solving strategies. Just as a skilled builder wouldn't use a hammer for every task, you shouldn't rely on a single teaching approach for every student or challenge.

Your toolbox will include:

- basics and fundamentals – securing strong foundations
- mathematical methods offering multiple pathways to solutions
- mathematical models – using visual and conceptual representations
- mathematical tools – from rulers and calculators to technology
- revision strategies to help learning stick
- exam techniques for turning knowledge into results.

Each chapter adds new tools to your kit, helping you build the flexibility and confidence to support every learner, whatever their starting point. This book will help you move students from 'I hate maths' to 'I can do this', with each chapter focusing on a key aspect of building mathematical resilience, from understanding why maths matters to developing effective revision strategies and exam techniques.

My strategies are grounded in research but designed for busy classrooms. You'll find:

- ready-to-use activities
- helpful scripts for tricky conversations
- adaptable approaches for different teaching contexts
- expert insights and teaching tips
- inclusive strategies for students with special educational needs and disabilities (SEND) and English as an additional language (EAL)
- reflection questions and clear next steps.

Whether you're new to supporting resistant learners or looking for fresh ideas, these approaches have all been used successfully with students who once believed

Grade 4 was out of reach. They're rooted in the work of experts like Dylan Wiliam, Malcolm Swan and Dr Steve Chinn, but translated into accessible, real-world practice.

What makes this book different is its focus on students' strengths. It's emotionally aware, culturally responsive and inclusive by design, written by a practising teacher for fellow teachers, with realistic expectations at its heart.

Getting started

Turning resistance into resilience begins with small, meaningful moments, such as when a student finally connects with a concept or sees how maths relates to their personal goals. Your role is to create those moments and provide support. You don't need to be a maths expert to make these strategies work; what matters most is believing in your students' capacity for growth, being open to trying new approaches and having patience! We know that mistakes are essential steps in the learning process. The real question isn't whether students *can* learn maths but how we can help them discover the ways that work for them.

Part One

Understanding Resistance

Chapter 1
'I Hate Maths!': What's Your Answer?

You rarely hear someone say, 'I hate reading' or 'I hate writing'; there's a stigma attached to that. You'd be shocked to hear someone admit they *can't* read. But it's perfectly acceptable to declare 'I don't do maths' or 'I'm not a maths person', as if our mathematical ability is a fixed state.

As a teacher, you'll see this play out daily. There's the student who exclaims, 'I hate maths!' before even sitting down, the one who mutters 'I'm just like my mum, I don't do maths!' and those quiet students who give up before they've even had a chance to try. Each of these presents a challenge and an opportunity for growth.

Understanding why students resist maths

Why is struggling with maths more socially acceptable than struggling with reading? It's partly because basic literacy is seen as essential, while mathematical ability is often viewed – wrongly – as a niche or innate talent rather than a skill everyone can achieve (Kowsun, 2004).

Many students have also faced years of accumulated setbacks that convinced them they don't belong in mathematical spaces. Some encountered teaching approaches that didn't click, others internalised cultural messages about who's 'naturally good' at maths. For students facing economic challenges, maths can feel tied to financial stress. Those with (potentially undiagnosed) learning differences often think, 'I'm not smart' rather than 'I process information differently'.

What resistance looks like

It's easy to misread people. What looks like defiance might be your student trying to protect themselves from failing in front of others. If someone seems disengaged, they might actually be overwhelmed or struggling to process what's happening.

Understanding these underlying factors helps us move beyond surface behaviours to make meaningful change.

Traditional classroom training often focuses on the most visible signs of mathematical resistance: dramatic outbursts, clear avoidance behaviours or students who simply give up. In post-16 settings, non-attendance is a common avoidance tactic.

Sometimes resistance speaks in code:

- 'I'm too tired' (a student who was up late caring for younger siblings)
- 'I knew it yesterday but I've forgotten' (someone whose working memory is overwhelmed)
- 'Can I go to the toilet?' (repeated requests when anxiety peaks)
- 'This is boring' (a student who's terrified of getting it wrong).

These are all messages about deeper needs. Neurodivergent students (those with attention deficit hyperactivity disorder (ADHD), autism or dyscalculia) may seem fine outwardly but struggle to follow instructions or manage sensory input, making it hard to keep up with the lesson. Sometimes cultural differences clash with classroom methods or prior learning, and EAL learners face the double challenge of decoding both the maths and the words at the same time.

When resistance becomes anxiety

Research shows that past negative experiences really influence students' views of their maths abilities. Eighty per cent of people have never heard the term 'maths anxiety' (Maths Anxiety Trust, 2018), but around 36 per cent of 15–26 year-olds in the UK experience it, affecting not just maths but wider areas of education and life as well (Pearson, n.d.). This prevalence gives us an opportunity to open conversations with students who might be relieved to know their feelings are shared by others.

National Numeracy, a charity devoted to everyday maths, has identified warning signs that indicate when simple dislike turns into anxiety:

- feeling panicked/stressed
- struggling to concentrate
- physical symptoms like increased heart rate, sweating, nausea, tears
- actively avoiding situations involving maths.

For students with SEND, anxiety may manifest through intense physical responses (outbursts, shutdowns or stimming behaviours) or non-verbal cues. You need to become a skilled observer rather than relying solely on what students tell you.

Confidence builder: Spotting anxiety

It's completely normal to feel unsure about recognising maths anxiety. The good news is, you don't need to be an expert to start noticing it. Small changes in behaviour can be clues: a student going quiet, fidgeting more than usual, avoiding eye contact or suddenly needing a break during maths.

Here are a few simple ways to tune in:

- Be curious. Ask privately: 'How do you feel when we start maths?' You don't need to have the perfect words, but showing interest opens up a conversation.
- Notice patterns. If someone regularly forgets equipment or asks to leave the room during maths, it might be more than coincidence.
- Listen. Phrases like 'I'm rubbish at this' or 'I'll never get it' often signal deeper anxiety.

Trust your instincts. If something feels off, it probably is. You don't need to diagnose, just be empathetic.

Remember, your response matters more than spotting every sign. A calm, supportive approach makes a huge difference. If you're ever concerned about more serious anxiety, reach out to your special educational needs coordinator (SENCo) or pastoral team. You're not alone in this.

Transforming resistance through your response

Take a moment to think about how you typically respond when a student says they hate maths. Your reaction can reinforce resistance or begin to shift it. Often, it's not just what you say but how you frame the conversation that follows: your tone, your curiosity and your willingness to listen all lay the groundwork for resilience.

Building rapport through discussion

Malcolm Swan's research shows that understanding in mathematics develops through discussion. By starting a dialogue instead of brushing off students' concerns, we're already tackling one of the biggest barriers to engagement (Swan, 2006). Our initial goal is to understand their emotional relationship with maths and start rebuilding it.

Script box: Building rapport

Having a pre-meditated response helps. When a student says: 'I hate maths!':

- Say this: 'That's a shame. What happened to make you feel that way?'
- Not this: 'Well, you need to pass it to get your qualification.'
- Follow-up: 'Lots of my students have felt that way at first, but we've found strategies that really help. Let's figure out what works for you.'

Remember, you're not trying to fix resistance instantly – just keep the conversation open.

Hear from the expert: Julia Smith, AQA maths expert panel member

'Whenever I hear someone say "I hate maths!" my response is one of the following: "Well you didn't have me as your maths teacher before so we're going to be fine!" or "Well, I hate ironing but I can still do it… you're going to be fine!" Be the *positivity* they need. If you're upbeat, they're more likely to be too'.

Once you've built rapport, gently challenge the idea that some people aren't 'maths people'. This is a mindset shaped by past struggles, but there's no such thing as being born good or bad at maths; it's a skill that grows through teaching, practice and persistence (Parker, 2015). Help students see that progress is possible, and that their past doesn't define their potential.

Script box: Challenging fixed mindsets

When a student says: 'I'm just not a maths person':

- Say this: 'Research shows there's no such thing as a "maths person", it's all about finding the way that works for you. Which parts of maths do you find most difficult?'
- Not this: 'You just need to try harder.'
- Follow-up: 'Let's focus on those specific areas and find methods that make more sense to you.'

Finding alternative pathways

Sometimes when the direct approach isn't clicking, it helps to explore what students are already good at. Asking, 'What do you love to do?' shifts the conversation from maths to personal interests, and then you can dive into how they developed those skills. It usually boils down to practice and learning from mistakes, meaning students already have the key skills for doing well in maths. Help them see that maths isn't so different from other skills.

The activities that follow are designed to work for all students, with built-in adaptations that don't single anyone out. Instead of creating separate versions for SEND or EAL learners, they offer multiple pathways that naturally support different needs, communication preferences and life experiences within the same framework.

Classroom activity: Postcard pedagogy

This activity invites students to explore their relationship with maths and consider what success means to them. It's designed to help them see that their experiences are not only valid, but shared by others: the real power of the exercise lies not just in what they write, but in the moment they realise they're not alone.

1 Start by giving each student two postcards or sticky notes. On the first, ask them to express why they're in this class or how they feel about maths. They can respond through words, drawings, symbols or a mix of all three.

2 On the second card, invite them to reflect on what success would look like for them personally. This could be academic, emotional or something entirely different.

3 Once everyone has finished, collect the cards and display them in two separate sections: one for feelings and motivations and one for definitions of success.

4 Offer flexible tools like emoji stickers, coloured pencils or mind-mapping templates. For students who prefer to speak rather than write, provide audio options such as voice memos. EAL learners or those with communication challenges might benefit from peer interviews. Anonymous submission can help students be honest.

On the first set of postcards, you'll often find practical reasons like 'I didn't concentrate in school' or 'I was sick and missed a lot of classes,' alongside emotional responses such as 'My teacher didn't like me' or 'I just didn't understand.' When these experiences are shared and displayed, the isolation that accompanies struggles with maths starts to ease.

Figure 1.1 Sticky note board recording students' feelings about English and maths.

The second postcard lets students define success on their own terms. It might be achieving Grade 4, or it could be feeling more confident, progressing to the next level or even just finishing maths forever! This step bridges the gap between how they feel now and what's possible in the future, turning reflection into motivation.

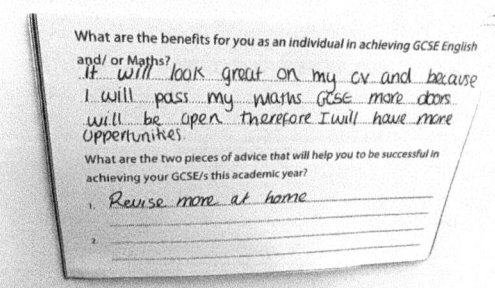

Figure 1.2 A student's response to what success will look like for them.

Figure 1.3 Students' sticky note responses.

Keep these postcards displayed on the wall, referring back to them regularly as reminders of why students are here and what they're working towards. Some schools turn them into posters.

Don't rush into problem-solving individual responses yet. The goal is to create a safe space for truth-telling and discovering common ground. Save specific support conversations for private moments, and use these collective insights to inform your overall approach.

Classroom activity: Learning lifeline

This activity helps students recognise their existing capabilities. From walking and talking to playing sports, they begin to see how they have consistently mastered complex skills over time.

1. Ask students to list *everything* they've learned since birth.
2. Create a timeline showing milestones from birth to age five, five to eleven, and eleven to present. They can draw or write about any skills, e.g. walking, talking, cycling, singing, drawing.
3. Discuss how they became skilled: it's all about practice!

Encourage them to think broadly. Almost anything is relevant: caring for siblings, developing self-advocacy skills, speaking multiple languages or being able to navigate new systems. Students who manage benefits, coordinate family schedules or help people with homework are already using thinking skills that transfer directly to formal maths.

Figure 1.4 A student's timeline of what they've learned since birth.

This activity isn't about false confidence, it's about recognising existing abilities and applying them to maths with the right support.

Teaching tip: Think wider

If students are struggling to see their strengths, suggest relatable role models (marathon runners, athletes, chefs or bilingual family members) who show how ordinary people develop skills through dedication.

Classroom activity: The alphabet of maths

Once students recognise their learning capacity, this activity helps them reconnect with mathematical concepts in a low-stakes way. Students are often surprised by how much vocabulary they already know.

1. Divide students into small groups and provide large whiteboards or paper to collaborate on.
2. Each group should come up with mathematical words from A to Z, adding little drawings to illustrate each one.
3. After 10 minutes, give groups one minute to 'borrow' ideas from each other.

This activity builds confidence, sparks discussion, promotes peer learning and creates a relaxed environment to help ease maths anxiety. Students often realise they know more about maths than they thought, and that mathematical language is all around them rather than entirely foreign! Use this as a springboard for discussion: add explanations, invite comments and support students in developing their ability to communicate mathematically.

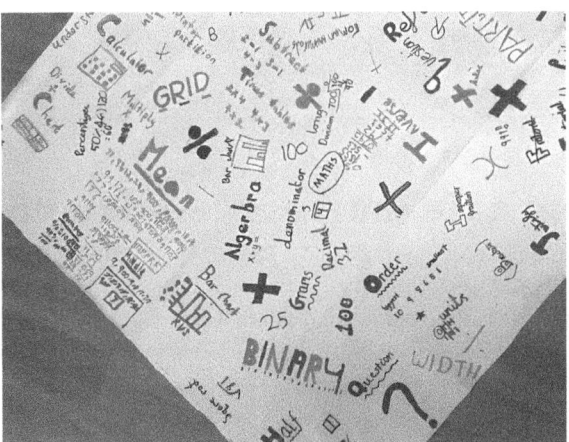

Figure 1.5 A maths alphabet.

Building confidence daily

These initial activities open the door to mathematical engagement, but the shift from resistance to resilience takes time. Real transformation happens through consistent, small interactions rather than one big moment.

When students encounter challenges during regular lessons, have a plan that helps maintain momentum:

- Acknowledge their struggle: 'I can see this is tough right now'.
- Offer choices: let students approach problems in different ways or control their pace.
- Remind them of past successes: 'Remember how well you handled fractions yesterday?'
- Break down complex problems into smaller, manageable steps.
- Follow up privately after tough lessons to offer support.

Teaching tip: The two-minute reset

If you spot anxiety kicking in, call for a reset.

- Everyone should stop what they're doing and take a quick stretch, wiggle or breath.
- Ask, 'What's one thing you're definitely confident with so far?'
- Start again from that point.

Anxious students need reminding of what they can do before tackling what they can't.

Creating safe learning environments

All of this contributes to a classroom where students feel safe being open about their maths challenges. It fosters a culture that embraces mistakes as part of learning, echoing Malcolm Swan's principles of maths instruction where, instead of seeing struggle as a sign of failure, we emphasise that it's normal to find things tough at first. With the right support, persistence leads to progress.

Creating a safe learning environment also means being careful with the language we use. Professor Steve Chinn tells us that the way we speak to students (especially during moments of difficulty) can either reinforce their confidence or deepen their anxiety. Small shifts in phrasing make a big difference in how students see themselves and their abilities, so try out the alternatives below.

Instead of...	Try...
You got it wrong.	Let's see what happened here.
You should know this.	Let's remind ourselves of this.
This is easy.	This gets easier with practice.
You're not trying.	What's making this feel hard right now?
Let's try with a simple one first.	Let's try with this one first.

Celebrate all efforts. Positive reinforcement helps students feel seen and valued for their thinking, not just their answers. Try phrases like:

- 'I love that you tried a different approach!'
- 'Mistakes help me understand your thinking.'
- 'You're really good at spotting patterns!'
- 'Your logical thinking was great there!'

Supporting all learning needs

Transforming your language is a good first step, but supporting mathematical confidence also means recognising and responding to the different learning needs in your classroom.

Every student comes with their own unique processing needs, cultural backgrounds and past experiences. Students learning English while tackling maths face an extra challenge. People with dyscalculia often struggle to retain certain facts, and those with attention challenges often struggle in traditional classroom setups. Luckily, simple changes can really help:

- give more time for questions
- add visual aids to verbal instructions
- offer different ways to show understanding
- for those who find it hard to express themselves verbally, provide alternatives like drawing, writing or using visual scales
- use tools such as Bouncy Balls (see Further Reading and Resources) or kitchen timers as classroom management tools (see Chapter 12).

Supporting students who say they hate maths isn't about having all the answers. It's about showing up with empathy, curiosity and a willingness to try something different. Every conversation, every small shift in language and every inclusive activity helps build the trust and resilience that students need to re-engage. As you move forward, keep your focus on what students *can* do, and use the tools in this book to help them see it too. The revolution starts with you.

Adapting to your setting

- **GCSE classrooms:** Focus on building confidence before addressing content gaps. Use peer support extensively and connect maths to post-16 opportunities and progression.
- **Resit students:** Acknowledge past difficulties without dwelling on them. Emphasise fresh starts and new approaches.
- **Vocational support contexts:** Make explicit connections between maths and students' chosen fields. Use industry-relevant examples.
- **One-to-one intervention:** Build strong relationships before pushing mathematical boundaries. Let students set their own pace.

Key research points

- Malcolm Swan: *Improving Learning in Mathematics* (2005)
  - Key takeaway: Understanding comes through discussion.
  - Use it: Build structured discussion opportunities into every lesson to reveal thought processes.
- Dr Steve Chinn: *Mathematics Anxiety in Secondary Students* (2019)
  - Key takeaway: Anxiety leads to withdrawal from learning.
  - Use it: Watch for signs of avoidance, address emotional needs before content and create low-stakes environments.
- Mathematical Anxiety research
  - Key takeaway: Many students mask mathematical difficulties as behavioural issues.
  - Use it: Look beyond surface behaviours to understand emotional responses to challenges.

Reflection questions

- When students say they don't like maths, how do I usually respond? What impact might my tone, body language and choice of words have on their confidence? How could I reframe my responses to build resilience and keep the conversation open?

- What signs of hidden resistance or anxiety might I be missing in my current students? How can I become more observant of subtle cues and what strategies could I use to respond with empathy?
- How do my own experiences with maths shape the way I react to student resistance? Do I project my past struggles or successes onto my learners? How can I ensure my personal history supports rather than limits my approach?
- What can I do to create the safest possible learning environment for my most anxious students?

Next steps

1 Try the *Postcard Pedagogy* activity with your next new group of students. Pay attention both to what they write and to how they respond to seeing others' experiences.
2 Keep a log of phrases students use to express resistance (e.g., 'I'm just not a maths person.', 'This is pointless.', 'I'll never use this.'). Group them into categories (e.g., confidence issues, relevance doubts, past trauma) and use this information to develop targeted responses.
3 Role-play with colleagues or rehearse during planning time to build fluency.

Chapter 2
Maths is Good for You!

From 'Why do I need this?' to 'I can see the benefits'

I don't need maths, Miss. My dad left school at 15 and he's doing fine. He runs his own building company now!

This statement, delivered with the confidence of someone who believes they've just won the argument, is one of the most common challenges we face. Students often point to successful people in their lives who seem to have 'made it' without maths, creating what feels like an unwinnable debate. How do you respond without dismissing their family members or contradicting lived experience?

The answer lies not in arguing against their observation, but in helping them see what's hidden in plain sight. That student's dad uses Pythagorean relationships through the 3-4-5 rule to ensure walls are square. He calculates material quantities for accurate job quotes, manages profit margins and tax obligations, and applies mathematical thinking to project timelines and resource allocation. The maths is there; it's just not labelled as such.

This chapter transforms the resistant question 'Why do I need this?' into genuine understanding of mathematical value. We'll move beyond forced relevance (those artificial connections that make students roll their eyes) to applications that resonate with their real aspirations and experiences.

Make the benefits concrete

Start with facts that matter to students, presented in ways that feel real, not theoretical. Research shows that people with strong numerical skills can earn up to £150,000 more over their working lifetime (Gov.uk, 2025). But that's just a number until we can make it personal.

Transform the research into language that resonates: 'That's enough for a flat in our area,' or 'That could buy a new car every three years of your working life,' or 'That's £3,000 extra every year for 50 years of working.' The more specific and relevant to their circumstances, the more impact the information will have.

> **Teaching tip: Making statistics personal**
>
> Don't just quote figures. Ask students: 'What would you do with an extra £3,000 every year?' Let them calculate what that means for their goals – holidays, cars, house deposits, supporting family. When they do the maths themselves, the benefits become real.

But earnings are just the beginning. Research tells us that people with strong numerical skills also:

- make better health decisions by understanding medical statistics, medication dosages and nutritional information (National Numeracy, 2018)
- make smarter financial choices because they grasp interest rates, insurance terms and investment returns (Al-Tamimi and Kadiyala, 2025)
- raise more mathematically confident children by supporting homework and modelling positive attitudes toward numbers (National Numeracy, 2024).

The research tells us that students will have better health choices, be able to make better life decisions and have better-educated children. They will also be able to help their own children with their maths homework when the time comes, which 20 per cent of parents currently avoid altogether (Open University Business School, 2019). When recruiting, employers primarily shortlist candidates with good maths (and English) qualifications on their CV (Gov.uk, 2013).

Being confident with maths helps protect you from being taken advantage of, too. If you understand percentages, you're less likely to fall for dodgy adverts that twist the numbers (Lusardi and Mitchell, 2014). If you get how probability works, you can judge risks more sensibly (Gigerenzer, 2014). And if you're clued up on statistics, you're better able to question what you see in the news, rather than taking it all at face value (Wuttke, 2014).

So the benefits of maths are wide-ranging and deeply personal. Numeracy matters. But what happens when students don't get the chance to access those benefits? When the system doesn't support them to succeed in maths, the consequences can be life-altering. And that's where the real challenge lies.

The current picture

Currently, students without a Grade 4 in GCSE maths must study the subject until 18, but education leaders and the Department for Education (DfE) are calling for more flexible, inclusive alternatives to the current resit system, which many believe isn't working for persistent strugglers (Department for Education, 2024). The majority of school leavers who fail to achieve Grade 4 will go on to resit, most at Foundation Tier, as this is considered a better exam experience than Higher Tier. The general consensus among FE leaders, practitioners and exam boards is that unless a student is likely to achieve Grade 6 at a resit, they should sit the Foundation Tier.

There is some encouraging news: the Survey of Adult Skills shows that young people aged 16–24 have made dramatic improvements in literacy and numeracy – literacy scores up seven per cent and numeracy up nine per cent (National Foundation for Educational Research, 2024). The 16–19 funding condition, introduced in 2014, has supported around 3 million young people over the past decade, particularly those lower-attaining students who need to continue with English and maths (Department for Education, 2024).

But here's the reality that keeps me awake at night: while we celebrate these overall improvements, we're still failing the students who need us most. The bottom ten per cent of learners remain significantly behind. Department for Education data shows that those with the lowest prior attainment at 16 are significantly less likely to achieve Level 3 qualifications by age 19 (Department for Education, 2024). And as the Curriculum and Assessment Review confirmed, students with lower GCSE grades at 16 were markedly less likely to progress to higher-level study or complete Level 3 qualifications by 19 (Department for Education, 2023). That gap isn't closing fast enough—and it matters.

These aren't just statistics, they're the faces we see in our classrooms every day. Rates of students who become Not in Education, Employment or Training (NEET) between 16 and 18 sit stubbornly at 12–15 per cent between 2012 and 2023 (Office for National Statistics, 2024). They're more likely to be disadvantaged or have additional learning needs, and frankly, we're not serving them well enough.

It's frustrating that the system's 'flexibilities', meant to help, still let too many students slip through the cracks. When I work with these students, I see their potential, but the system often fails to support it. This is why the approaches in this book matter. Every student in that bottom ten per cent deserves better than becoming another NEET statistic.

Real stories, real struggles, real success

While the structure of post-GCSE maths education may evolve, the core principle remains unchanged: strong maths skills unlock better opportunities. Whether through revised qualifications, alternative pathways or more tailored teaching, the need to build mathematical confidence and competence is more urgent than ever.

That's why it's important to share success stories: examples that show students it's possible to struggle and still succeed. Like Lauren Reid from City College Plymouth, who achieved Grade 4 on her ninth attempt to get into university and study occupational therapy (TES, 2019). Or Jess Ward, who passed on her fourth attempt and went from learning support assistant to aspiring teacher (BBC, 2023). Find local stories that normalise the struggle with maths. One of them may even be your own.

Revealing the maths behind every pathway

One of the strongest barriers to mathematical engagement stems from the persistent myth that 'creative' or 'practical' careers don't require maths. Addressing this misconception doesn't just improve engagement – it opens doors students don't even realise are shut yet!

> ### Case study: Transforming career assumptions
>
> One of my Year 11 students was convinced her dream of becoming a beautician didn't require maths. 'I'm creative, not mathematical,' she said, skipping lessons whenever possible. Instead of arguing, I asked her to explore the maths behind running a salon. She soon discovered it involved profit margins, staff commissions, appointment scheduling and ratios for colour mixing. A real-life visit revealed spreadsheets for stock control, pricing and customer trends. Within a month, her attitude had shifted to: 'I didn't realise being good at business meant being good at maths.' The key was letting her uncover those connections herself.

These applications often operate invisibly but they're critical. A restaurant that miscalculates portion costs might lose customers or money. A mechanic who misjudges timing could damage an engine. Maths is everywhere, it just isn't always labelled.

> ### Teaching tip: Student-led career exploration
>
> Rather than *telling* students about mathematical applications, get them to discover these connections themselves. Ask them to research the maths involved in their dream careers. You'll be surprised how many applications they uncover.

> ### Classroom activity: Household maths interview
>
> Ask students to interview people close to them about how they use maths in work and daily life. Use the prompts to spark conversations.
>
> - What calculations do you do regularly at home or at work?
> - What mathematical mistakes could cause serious problems in your job?
> - Do you use estimation and approximation in your daily life?
> - What mathematical skills do you wish you'd developed better at school?
> - When do you notice yourself thinking mathematically without realising it?
>
> This exercise reveals that people use more maths than students realise, again challenging the myth that mathematics isn't needed in 'real' jobs. It also opens up intergenerational conversations about learning and work, which can help motivate students further.

The compound effect

Maths skills build on each other, unlocking future opportunities students may not yet see. When students start to see maths in everyday life, it stops being just about exams. It becomes a tool for understanding the world – from money and health to gaming and careers. The challenge is helping them see it.

- **Financial literacy:** Students face complex financial maths daily. Mobile contracts require comparing pricing structures and long-term costs. Choosing energy suppliers means interpreting unit rates and standing charges. Credit decisions involve interest and total cost calculations. Without these skills, students risk costly mistakes lasting years.

- **Health and fitness:** Maths is central to health goals. Body mass index (BMI) helps interpret health assessments; dosage calculations ensure safe treatment. Calorie and macronutrient tracking supports strength building and weight management. Fitness apps like Strava use data analysis. Students who dislike maths often engage with it here because it matters to them.

- **Technology and gaming:** Digital life is full of maths. Algorithms shape social media; online security involves probability and risk. Games use stats, optimisation and resource management – some even involve topology. Students who resist classroom maths often embrace complex thinking through game mechanics.

Making these connections explicit helps combat disengagement because they're rooted in real life, not contrived textbook examples. Often, students dismiss maths as irrelevant because they fear failure (it's easier to say 'I'll never need this' than admit anxiety). Recognising this defence mechanism lets us respond with empathy and practical support.

Script box: Making maths relevant

When a student says: 'I'll never use equations in real life':

- Say this: 'You're probably right – you won't be solving quadratics at the supermarket. But learning how to work with them builds logical thinking and problem-solving skills you'll use everywhere. And they pop up in surprising places, like analysing house prices, studying viruses or working with scientific data.'
- Not this: 'You never know when you might need them.'
- Follow-up: 'What careers or activities are you interested in? Let's look at the mathematical thinking they actually use.'

Teaching tip

Explore posters from Maths Careers (see Further Reading and Resources). Resources like 'When will I ever need this?' and 'What's the point of Pythagoras?' show how maths links to real life and careers (see Chapter 7).

Classroom activity: Maths in the news

Bring in headlines or articles on house prices, polling data, health studies, environmental stats or footballers' wages (men and women). Ask students to identify the maths involved and what questions they'd ask about the data.

This exercise shows that maths literacy is civic power, as it helps students question claims that affect their lives. Without it, they're vulnerable to manipulation by politicians, advertisers and media.

Maths anxiety and relevance

Maths shows up in unexpected places, but just recognising its importance doesn't always translate into confidence. For many students, especially those with a history of struggle, the issue isn't whether maths *matters*, it's whether they believe they can do it. That's where emotional readiness and psychological safety come in.

Dr Steve Chinn's extensive research on mathematical difficulties emphasises that students with mathematical anxiety often reject learning not because they can't understand, but because they don't see why they should try (Chinn, 2012). His work shows that addressing the 'why' before the 'how' significantly improves engagement. Students with dyscalculia and maths anxiety benefit particularly from seeing mathematics as a collection of useful tools rather than abstract concepts.

Confidence builder: When you're not sure how to respond

Teaching resistant learners is challenging, especially when you're still building confidence in your own strategies. In moments of uncertainty, having a few go-to responses can help you stay calm, supportive and constructive. Here are some simple, effective ways to respond when you're not sure what to say.

- Start with curiosity: 'Tell me more about that' gives you space to process the situation while showing you're open and interested.
- Acknowledge their feelings: 'It sounds like maths has been really frustrating for you.' Validating their experience helps build trust and lowers emotional defences.
- Ask for their ideas: 'What do you think might help?' often produces surprising insights.
- Buy yourself thinking time: 'That's a really important point – let me think about the best way to help with that.' This shows respect for their concern while giving you space to reflect or seek support.

And remember: sometimes you won't know – and that's okay. My stock response in those moments? 'I'm not Carol Vorderman either! It's okay to forget things or get them wrong – what matters is double-checking your work and being able to spot when something doesn't look right.' This kind of honesty normalises uncertainty and models that growth mindset. It also reinforces the idea that maths isn't about perfection – it's about persistence, reflection and learning.

Value, belief and effort

Activities like maths in the news and talking about maths relevance work because they target three essentials for success identified by National Numeracy: value, belief and effort (National Numeracy, 2017).

- **Value:** show why maths matters – link it to careers, earnings and life skills.
- **Belief:** build confidence through small wins and celebrate progress.
- **Effort:** make participation feel worthwhile – maths isn't a spectator sport.

When students see value and believe they can succeed, they take ownership. Your role is to support that shift. As Dylan Wiliam notes, the most powerful learning happens when students become architects of their own learning – the more they do for themselves, the faster they improve (Wiliam, 2011).

Letting students find the maths

One of the best ways to show maths matters is through guided discovery. When students uncover applications themselves, they're more likely to remember them. Ask them to track every mathematical decision in a day, e.g. choosing the fastest route, planning timings, checking if they have enough money for lunch or working out wages and tips. Even discount cards can spark thinking about budgeting, savings and percentages. After the audit, ask students: 'Which of these decisions surprised you as being mathematical?' Then connect their discoveries to curriculum content:

- route planning → networks and algorithms
- time management → ratios and proportions
- budgeting → percentages, decimals and financial literacy.

Maths isn't just something done in class, it's a tool your students already use to navigate their world.

> **Classroom activity: Future planning**
>
> Ask students to imagine their ideal life in ten years' time: where they'll live, the work they'll do, goals they want to achieve, even problems they'd like to solve. Then work backwards: What steps will get them there? What skills will they need? How could maths support those ambitions, even in ways that aren't obvious at first?

Addressing relevance

Students sometimes resist maths because of the messages they receive from their families or communities. In some households, maths isn't seen as essential. A student might say, 'My mum says I don't need maths because she never used it.' This belief deserves respect, but we can gently broaden their view.

A thoughtful response might acknowledge that their mum made things work in her own way, then explain that today's job market demands different skills. Frame maths as a way to open up more options rather than contradicting the parent. This approach respects family values while encouraging new possibilities. Positive family engagement shifts attitudes, too. One Year 11 student of mine, Alice, said, 'Miss, you phoned my mum last night about my maths!' When I told her it was to share what she had done really well in maths , she replied, 'She was chuffed, Miss! I only usually get bad phone calls.'

But family influence isn't the only barrier. Increasingly, students question the relevance of maths because they believe technology has made it redundant. Students often argue, 'Why learn this when my phone can do it?' Reframe the conversation: it's not about doing the calculation, it's about understanding what the technology is doing. Mathematical literacy means knowing when to use tools, how to interpret results, and whether they make sense. A calculator can give an answer, but only understanding can tell you if it's right.

Script box: Technology and mathematical understanding

When a student says: 'Why do I need to learn this? My phone can do it for me.'

- Say this: 'True, your phone can do the calculation. But you still need to know what to ask it, and whether the answer makes sense.'
- If they say: 'But it's always right, isn't it?'
- Tell them: 'Only if you put the right numbers in. If you're working out a 15 per cent tip on a £47 meal and your phone says £43 would you spot that something's off? Your maths skills help you catch mistakes and make smart decisions.'

Having ready-made responses like this helps you show students that maths and technology work together, not in competition. When they understand how and why maths works, they're not just better at using tools, they're more confident in their own thinking. That confidence often sparks a wider shift in how they approach learning overall.

The confidence cycle

Mathematical confidence creates a ripple effect beyond the subject. When students feel capable, they become more persistent, embrace challenge, and see mistakes as part of learning. Assessment plays a key role here: focusing on application, reasoning and real-world problem solving shows that maths is about thinking, not just correctness.

Try approaches such as:

- **real-world problems:** use scenarios students might genuinely face
- **explanation and communication:** ask them to explain reasoning and link it to practical contexts
- **choice and agency:** offer options for demonstrating understanding
- **recognition of the process:** reward mathematical thinking, not just final answers.

> **Teaching tip: Make value visible**
>
> Start each topic by showing its real-world relevance. Use examples from students' interests, career goals or everyday challenges. Bring in guest speakers or short vlogs to show how maths is used in fields from mechanics to makeup artistry.

Students don't need to love maths to benefit from it – but they do need to see why it matters. Our role is to make that value clear, authentic and connected to what they care about.

Adapting to your setting

- **GCSE classrooms:** Link topics to careers; use guest speakers or vlogs.
- **Resit students:** Focus on practical applications and progression routes.
- **Vocational support contexts:** Connect maths directly to chosen fields.
- **One-to-one intervention:** Personalise links to individual goals.

Key research points

- National Numeracy: *Measuring Mathematical Resilience* (2018)
  - Key takeaway: Success requires value, belief and effort.
  - Use it: Begin each topic by discussing its value, build belief through accessible entry points and make effort feel worthwhile.

- Robey & Jones: *Engaging Learners in GCSE Maths and English* (2015)
  - Key takeaway: Barriers include past negative experiences, lack of relevance and low self-belief.
  - Use it: Create new positive experiences, connect content to relevance, and build belief through small wins.
- Dr Steve Chinn: *Mathematics Anxiety in Secondary Students* (2019)
  - Key takeaway: Students engage better when maths is framed as a useful tool.
  - Use it: Present maths as a way to solve problems students care about.
- Dylan Wiliam: *Embedded Formative Assessment* (2009)
  - Key takeaway: Students become architects of their own learning when they understand its purpose.
  - Use it: Always explain why a concept matters before teaching how to use it.

Reflection questions

- How clearly do I connect maths learning to my students' goals and interests?
- Which mathematical applications are most relevant to my students' lives?
- How can I help students see maths as a form of empowerment, not just a requirement?
- What evidence can I offer to show the real-world value of mathematical literacy?

Next steps

- Use quick questionnaires, informal chats or tools like Google Forms or Padlet to learn about hobbies, career goals and challenges. Ask:
  - What job would you love to have one day?
  - What subjects or activities do you enjoy most?
  - What problems in the world would you like to help solve?
- Find out what maths different careers use – budgeting for event planning, measurements in construction, data analysis in marketing. Use job profiles and career sites, or invite professionals to share real examples. Create short 'maths in the real world' spotlights for class.
- Ask students to explore how maths appears in everyday life – budgeting, shopping, cooking or managing time. This builds connections to their lived experience.

Chapter 3
Motivation: Moving People to Action

From 'I don't see the point' to 'I want to keep learning'

Whenever I lead a session for teachers focused on continued professional development (CPD), I start by asking 'What do you want to get out of this session?' One of the most common responses is, 'Help me motivate students who seem unmotivated.' They've tried everything – rewards, consequences, real-world links – yet still face late arrivals, reluctant participation and the familiar question: 'When will I ever use this?' with genuine exasperation rather than curiosity.

The word 'motivation' comes from the Latin *motivus* – 'a moving cause', the force that drives action. But what moves a student who's faced years of perceived failure? How do we create momentum when past efforts brought only frustration and anxiety? And how do we spark curiosity in learners who've learned to protect themselves by not caring?

For resit students, the challenge is even greater. Poor attendance often compounds low confidence, and many see maths as a barrier to their real goals. They carry the weight of public failure: everyone knows they didn't achieve a Grade 4 pass the first time. Yet within this challenge lies real opportunity. These learners often have resilience, persistence and problem-solving skills from other areas of life (see Chapters 1 and 2). Our job isn't to create motivation from nothing – it's to redirect those strengths toward maths while removing the barriers that blocked success.

Understanding the motivation puzzle

Picture a Year 11 student on the Grade 3/4 borderline. When extra revision sessions are announced, they just shrug. The drive to push through has faded. They've seen enough maths to reach a Grade 4 (maybe even a 5) – it's just that they can't do it all, and so determination has turned into resignation. This scene plays out in classrooms across the country every spring. But the challenge isn't knowledge, it's motivation. Most students know more than they think.

At the time of writing (January 2026), students who don't achieve at least a Grade 4 in English and/or maths still have to retake the exams. This has been highly controversial (Tes reporter, 2025). Try teaching students who don't want to be there … and often aren't. Headteacher unions have called it a 'remorseless treadmill of demotivating resits', and schools and colleges feel the strain on time, staffing and resources (Busby, 2024). This policy is under review following the government's Curriculum and Assessment Review (DfE, 2025), so changes may be on the horizon.

Research from the Education Policy Institute (EPI) also shows the picture is far from equal. Disadvantaged students, on average, achieve one-eighth of a grade lower than their more affluent peers in maths resits (EPI, 2025). Regional differences also stand out: the north west performs particularly well, thanks in part to strong collaboration and shared practice among providers.

Gender adds another layer. Boys tend to make more progress in maths resits – almost a quarter of a grade more than girls. The gender gap in maths is already nearly five times bigger than in English, so this isn't new, but it's stubborn. Why? One reason might be numbers: more boys resit maths, so the overall improvement appears greater. However, this does not change the fact that girls are being left behind.

So what does this mean for us in the classroom? It means being intentional. Build confidence, especially for female learners. Share female role models and STEM stories. Create safe spaces where mistakes are normal and effort is celebrated. Keep disadvantaged learners front and centre with structured revision, clear routines and strong relationships. Motivation grows when students feel supported and believe they can succeed.

Looking ahead, FFT Education Datalab (an independent research organisation) is tracking the first fully post-pandemic cohort, with added extra curriculum time for resit groups. Will it work? Pass rates remain low. In summer 2024, just 17.4 per cent of students achieved a Grade 4 in GCSE maths resits (Joint Council for Qualifications, 2024). But the several thousands of people who do succeed show the resit policy can raise attainment by age 25. For many borderline Year 11 students, though, the mindset is often: 'It's okay, I'll just take it again at college'. When the pressure builds, it's easy for them to switch off. In my classroom, rather than a co-constructed set of classroom rules, I kept it simple with just two: 'Be kind' and 'Work hard'.

Traditional motivation strategies often fail because they assume students should want to learn maths for its own sake. As one student said: 'Miss, will you stop doing maths to me? You know I hate it!' Motivation isn't something we do to students – it comes when conditions support their need for competence, autonomy and connection.

Understanding what's behind 'unmotivated' students

Motivation and engagement are constant challenges in maths teaching, especially for students who find the subject hard or unappealing. But 'unmotivated' rarely tells the whole story. When a student seems disengaged, ask: 'What's driving this? Are they protecting themselves from failure? Overwhelmed by the gap between where they are and where they need to be?' What looks like resistance is often self-preservation. A shrug, a blank stare or 'I don't care' can be a shield against more disappointment.

Professor Reinhard Pekrun (University of Essex) reminds us that emotions drive learning. A little anxiety before an exam can help if balanced with optimism. He also highlights emotional contagion: *our* mood matters (Pekrun, 2025). When we ourselves bring energy and genuine enjoyment of maths, students often mirror it. Motivation isn't just cognitive, it's emotional.

Hidden barriers

Disengagement in the maths classroom often conceals deeper, less visible struggles. Robey and Jones (2015) highlight how students may face a range of barriers that go unnoticed unless we look closely.

Some challenges stem from unmet or misunderstood learning needs. A student with dyslexia might avoid maths because word problems feel overwhelming and inaccessible. A learner with autism may find the unpredictability of classroom discussions unsettling, while a student with ADHD (so often labelled as disruptive) might just be trying to manage their need for movement and stimulation in an environment that doesn't accommodate it.

Other barriers lie beyond the classroom. For some students, disadvantage shapes their ability to engage. Homework might compete with caring responsibilities at home, or a part-time job may be essential to their family's income, leaving little time or energy for study. These pressures are rarely visible, but they have a profound impact.

> **Teaching tip: Reading the signs**
>
> Look for patterns rather than isolated incidents. Does a student disengage during specific topics? Do they thrive in discussion but struggle with written work? These often reveal the real barriers to learning.

As discussed earlier, behaviour is communication. When a student says 'I don't care' or disengages, they're often expressing something deeper. Our role is to decode that, not dismiss it.

Sustaining the work

Staying motivated through challenges is hard for students and teachers alike. Some days, staying positive takes real effort. When it feels tough, remember: we teach the students in front of us, not the ones we wish we had. Our role is to meet them where they are and help them take the next step.

Supporting resistant learners is deeply rewarding, but also emotionally demanding. Resistance may stir up personal memories or professional doubts. Recognising these moments helps us respond with empathy, not defensiveness. When a student says 'This is stupid', it's usually frustration, not a reflection on your teaching.

You don't have to do this alone. Lean on colleagues, learning support teams and professional communities. Mentoring, supervision and access to mental health support can make a real difference. Sustainable teaching means building networks that support both you and your students. Look at the successful resit outcomes in the North West.

Success stories

When motivation feels fragile, stories can reignite it. They show progress is possible even against the odds. Sharing them builds student confidence and reminds teachers that their work changes lives. Whether you're in a school or college, share your success stories. Think of former students who've achieved great things – ordinary or extraordinary. And don't forget the staff: do you have inspiring maths journeys to share?

Some stories make headlines. Lauren and Jess earned Grade 4 after multiple resits (see Chapter 2). A 92-year-old man sat the GCSE maths exam alongside his teenage friend (Daily Mail, 2022). Darren Hankey, now Principal of Hartlepool College, left school with three O-levels, resat maths at night school, passed, and unlocked a path to university, teaching and a Master's degree.

Many schools celebrate success visibly – with posters or life-size cut-outs of former students. Each one shares how maths opened doors:

> I wouldn't be a nurse if I hadn't gotten my Grade 4 in maths – I couldn't even start the training!

> I'm a pilot and I use maths every day – I absolutely couldn't do my job without it!

Celebrating success is a powerful antidote to detachment. Real stories chip away at the 'what's the point?' mindset. But what about students still absent in class? That's where we dig deeper, beyond labels, to what's really driving that disengagement.

Beyond the RHINO label: supporting genuine disengagement

Let's talk about the 'RHINO' analogy: students who are 'Really Here In Name Only' (Steward and Nardi, 2002). Research with Year 9s used this term for learners who attend but mentally check out. The perception that maths is difficult and boring persists (remember the 'I hate maths!' theme from Chapter 1). That mindset leads to students just going through the motions because they have to.

This challenge is even bigger in resit groups, where attendance is often a struggle. Ofsted flags this regularly, and getting students through the door takes real effort. Timetabling doesn't help when maths is slotted in at the end of the day or after long vocational sessions. Successful schools prioritise maths early, though that's not always practical. Some colleges even hire staff to call home daily for the first six weeks to reinforce that attendance isn't optional. It's expensive but it works.

We need to look beyond the label and understand what's really happening. When a student disengages, what's really going on?

Script box: Responding to disengagement

When you notice a student switching off:

- Say this: 'I've noticed you seem to be finding things tough lately. Can we have a chat about what might help?'
- Not this: 'You need to start paying attention and making more effort.'
- Follow-up: 'What's one thing that would make this easier for you right now?'

Growth mindset

So how do we re-engage students who've mentally switched off? One powerful approach is to shift the narrative from fixed ability to growth mindset. When students believe they *can* improve, even small wins start to matter. This mindset is especially vital during revision season, when pressure builds and motivation wavers. During these high-pressure moments, teacher encouragement – whether humorous or heartfelt – can make all the difference. Your answer to 'I hate maths!' could simply be 'for now'.

You might hear someone say, half-jokingly, 'What are we going to have to do so I don't have to see your face again next year – and you don't have to see mine? Much as I like you!' Or they'll remind students, 'Nobody ever went into an exam saying "Oh no, I revised too much!"' Others offer quiet encouragement: 'You worked hard and will get the grade you deserve', or a gentle reality check: 'You don't need 100 per cent to get a Grade 4… or even Grade 5!'

These comments reflect the pressure students are under and the creative ways teachers try to channel that pressure into action. Our role is to steer that energy in a positive direction.

> **Hear from the expert: Darren Hankey, Principal, Hartlepool College**
>
> 'I'm not in the business of dispensing "silver bullets" when it comes to getting reluctant learners through their resits in FE. It's hard work, it's a slog and it's a struggle. But as with most things in life, the basics will get any teacher a long way. For me, these are:
>
> 1 Having high expectations of all learners.
> 2 Structuring the curriculum so it builds knowledge and confidence.
> 3 Delivering high-quality teaching, learning and assessment practice.'

Building on Darren Hankey's focus on high expectations and strong foundations, we also need to help students develop the mindset and motivation to engage. Rather than framing resits as a threat, we can present the remaining time as an opportunity.

Dylan Wiliam reminds us that 'teachers do not create learning; only learners create learning' (Wiliam, 2009). Students must see themselves as active agents in their education, not passive recipients. That means giving them choices, encouraging self-assessment and making it clear that we're here to support, not control, their progress. Crucially, they need the motivation to drive this process themselves.

This is where Carol Dweck's concept of a growth mindset becomes powerful (Dweck, 2016). It has transformed how we think about motivation. Students who believe ability grows through effort and strategy are more resilient and willing to take on challenges. Those with a fixed mindset see ability as fixed and are more likely to give up.

How do we build this in our classrooms? Lots of small changes can make a huge difference. Change your language: praise students' effort and thinking strategies, not 'natural ability'. Normalise mistakes by making it clear that errors are part of learning, not proof of failure. Adopt mastery approaches, where everyone works on the same big ideas, but at different levels of complexity (this reinforces the belief that everyone can succeed, with persistence).

There's a wealth of CPD and resources on growth mindset. Explore, share and build your own strategies. This work can transform how students see themselves and what they believe they can achieve.

Why this matters post-COVID

The pandemic deeply disrupted maths learning. The Royal Society reports that over half of students are at least three months behind, with motivation hit hard (Royal Society, n.d.). Teachers say that lack of engagement was a bigger barrier than lack of technology. Add to that high staff absence and a sense of being undervalued, and the challenge is clear.

But here's the good news: small, consistent actions like building student ownership, fostering growth mindset and creating emotionally safe classrooms can make a big difference, even in tough contexts. One aim of this book is to address the issues COVID exposed. When schools reopened, teachers rightly focused on practical topics – constructions, calculators, graphs. But many students missed key experiences during lockdown. As a result, basic skills (using a protractor, ruler, compass, calculator, understanding money, telling the time) remain shaky. Exam technique is another area where this cohort struggles.

Curriculum content

By Year 11, students have already encountered enough maths content to achieve at least a Grade 4. For those resitting after a Grade 3, the issue isn't exposure, it's mastery. The challenge is cutting through the overwhelming curriculum and finding the right focus.

Concentrating on key parts of the curriculum and areas of difficulty, which you can identify using Examiners' Reports, and sharpening exam technique can make a real difference. With a targeted approach, it's entirely possible to move students from Grade 3 to 4 (and sometimes even to 5!) in the time available.

One effective approach is the 5Rs curriculum (see Chapter 12), designed for borderline Year 11 Foundation students and resitters. It narrows the curriculum to 40 high-frequency topics and builds in daily practice, exam technique and tool fluency. I talk about this in detail in my podcast with Craig Barton (see Further Resources and Reading). It resonates with teachers because it tackles the root causes of underperformance at Grade 4 and below.

The strength of the 5Rs lies in its simplicity and structure. It tackles the two biggest barriers for resit and borderline students: overwhelm and lack of focus. By narrowing the curriculum to the most frequently tested topics and embedding daily routines, it reduces cognitive load and builds confidence through repetition. Each step is designed to reinforce the last – recall strengthens memory, routine practice builds fluency, and exam-style questions develop technique.

Another approach, the Focused 15 curriculum developed by Emma Bell, zeroes in on 15 key areas where Grade 4 students can succeed and where Grade 3 students often struggle (Bell, 2020). By narrowing focus and strengthening these essential topics, the approach builds mastery and supports better outcomes.

Both frameworks are flexible, giving teachers autonomy over pacing and progression while maintaining a clear structure for targeted learning. While the

5Rs offer a structured daily rhythm across a broad set of high-frequency topics, the Focused 15 zooms in on the most impactful areas for borderline learners. Both approaches reduce overload and build confidence – but in slightly different ways.

> ### Hear from the Expert: Emma Bell, MEI
>
> 'The Focused 15 Framework demonstrates how focusing on the essential, transferable skills allows students to learn more by studying less, nurturing both motivation and success. Here's a simple, practical way to structure revision:
>
> - Start with strengths: Build on what students already understand to give them confidence and momentum.
> - Develop the connections: Focus on the links between concepts to deepen students' understanding.
> - Prioritise with purpose: Leave the less-connected content for later, once the essentials feel secure.

This approach reduces cognitive overload and builds momentum. Starting with what students know creates early wins, which boosts confidence and motivation. Tackling 'almost there' topics next maximises impact, while parking the hardest content prevents frustration and wasted time. It's about working smarter, not harder.

> ### Classroom activity: Revision cards
>
> Using revision flashcards can be an effective way for students to engage with the material. Here's how to implement it:
>
> 1. Give students a full set of revision cards covering the GCSE maths Foundation Tier curriculum.
> 2. Ask them to sort the cards into three piles:
>   - topics they know really well
>   - topics they know a bit about but need more practice
>   - topics they don't know at all.
> 3. Once they've sorted their cards, your students have made themselves a personalised action plan. They can focus on strengthening what they know, consolidate partial knowledge and avoid stressing over unfamiliar topics for now. This method builds confidence: there should be plenty in the first pile, a few in the second and the last pile can wait!

> **Teaching tip**
>
> Revision card sets are also available for the Higher Tier and work just as effectively. You can source these from organisations such as The Mathematical Association and Corbettmaths.

Encouraging self-directed study

Self-directed study builds that growth mindset. When students choose what, how, and when to study, they shift from passive compliance to active ownership. They learn that progress comes from effort, persistence and smart strategies.

Once students identify areas of confidence, encourage practice through games or exercises. Moving away from traditional homework reduces pressure and shifts focus to genuine learning. The message: *work because it helps you succeed, not because you're being monitored.*

Self-study can be tech- or paper-based, but games make it engaging. Here are three great mobile-friendly options (see Further Reading and Resources for URLs):

1. **Mathsbot.com, Fluent calculations:** This site, created by Jonny Hall, offers a fantastic range of exercises to build fluency in core skills like addition, subtraction, multiplication, division and percentages. Students can request hints and explore different approaches to calculations, which is especially helpful for those with SEND/additional learning support (ALS) needs. You can also adjust the number of questions to avoid overwhelm. All of Jonny Hall's resources (Do-Nows, Number of the Day and Nasty Negatives) are excellent for self-study.
2. **You can't do simple maths under pressure:** A fast-paced game by Tom Scott. Some students love the challenge; others find it intense. It's great for building speed and confidence.
3. **Transum games:** Offers a wide range of fun, accessible games and exercises for practice and consolidation – quick to access and ideal for revision on the go.

Making self-directed study accessible

To make self-directed study work for all learners, we need to consider their diverse needs.

For students with ADHD or attention difficulties, break tasks into five-minute chunks, use visual timers and build in movement breaks. Avoid overwhelming them with too many options – offer structured choices (e.g. two methods or three topics). For students with autism, predictability is key. Clear routines and visual schedules reduce anxiety and help them focus. Quiet, low-stimulation spaces also support concentration. Disadvantaged students may lack tech access or quiet study spaces. Prioritise mobile-friendly, offline-compatible resources, and offer supervised study time at school – it can be a lifeline.

> **Teacher tip: Printable and offline-friendly resources**
>
> - **Mathsbot.com** offers printable versions of many activities.
> - **30-second challenges** are great for building fluency quickly. You can find printable versions on TES and online.
> - **Crossnumber puzzles** – like crosswords but with numbers – are excellent for paper-based practice.
> - **MathShed**, curated by Graeme Andre, is a treasure trove of printable resources that support fluency and consolidation.
>
> By offering flexible formats and thoughtful adaptations, we can make self-directed study truly accessible.

Platforms like Mathsbot and Transum do more than deliver content – they open doors. Used thoughtfully, they support diverse learners by reducing barriers and offering flexible access.

- For students with dyslexia, features like text-to-speech, adjustable fonts and background colours (via site or browser settings) ease reading strain. Audio instructions help shift focus to the maths itself.

- Students with dyscalculia benefit from visual tools like number lines and manipulatives. Breaking problems into steps reduces cognitive load and builds confidence.

- For learners with EAL needs, visuals (diagrams, animations, interactive tasks) convey meaning beyond language. These platforms allow self-paced practice, repetition and gradual understanding. While cultural relevance varies, many global platforms aim to include familiar, engaging scenarios.

What matters most is that these tools give students a way in. They offer flexibility, choice and a sense of control – all qualities that support not just access, but agency.

> **Teaching tip: Put students into the moment of success**
>
> The video *The Day I Passed Maths* showcases a student proudly sharing his results with his dad. Think about the emotions in that moment – pride, relief, joy – and how we can create similar experiences for our students.

Adapting to your setting

- **GCSE classrooms:** Regular use of revision card sets – tailored for both Foundation and Higher Tier students – can help embed key concepts and build confidence over time.
- **Resit students:** The same card sets can support self-directed study, offering structure and direction without overwhelming them.
- **Vocational support contexts:** In these contexts it's often about shifting the narrative. Fostering positive conversations around the value of maths – and sharing success stories – can be incredibly motivating. When students see that others like them have succeeded, it helps them believe they can too.
- **One-to-one interventions:** Revision card sets can be used to build on what students already know. Focused practice and consolidation exercises help strengthen understanding and create a sense of progress.

Key research points

- Education Policy Institute: *English and Maths Resits: Drivers of Success*
    - Key outcomes: Difference in outcomes across different groups.
    - Use it: Consider disadvantaged students and gender disparity. Consider geographical difference in outcomes and reasons for these.
- Carol Dweck: *Growth Mindset*
    - Key takeaway: Growth mindset is a key to success.
    - Use it: Create dialogues and classroom experiences where students move from 'I cannot do this' to 'I cannot do this…yet'.
- The 5Rs curriculum and the Focused 15 approach
    - Key takeaway: Narrowing the curriculum to essential components with a mastery approach.
    - Use it: Consider each approach and use as appropriate to your setting.

Reflection questions

- How comfortable are you working with demotivated students? What strategies do you already use? What other support might help?
- Could you collaborate with colleagues to foster a growth mindset? Who does this particularly well in your setting?
- How do you feel about the idea of narrowing curriculum content? What questions or concerns does that raise for you?

Next steps

1 Start the conversation: Discuss growth mindset approaches with colleagues. What's already happening – and what else could be done?
2 Celebrate success: Identify and share your own success stories. Ask colleagues to do the same, and consider showcasing them – perhaps during a Maths Week event.
3 Explore resources: Try a range of practice and consolidation exercises with your students. Explore the world of Transum Games and Mathsbot (see Further Reading and Resources), and look out for printable options too.

Part Two

Building Foundations

Chapter 4

Mathematical Fluency and Core Skills

Building the foundation for mathematical confidence

Sir, I know I should be able to do 7 × 8 quickly, but I still have to count on my fingers. Everyone else just knows it.

This student highlights a key barrier to maths confidence: the gap between *understanding* and *automatic recall*. She grasps multiplication – can explain it, draw arrays and solve word problems – but when 7 × 8 appears inside an algebra or percentage question, her thinking stalls while she works out the arithmetic.

This isn't about intelligence, and it certainly isn't about mathematical ability. It's about developing the fluency that frees up working memory for higher-level thinking. Mathematical fluency is like reading fluency: when we struggle to decode individual words, we miss the meaning of the sentence. When students struggle with basic mathematical facts, complex problem solving becomes overwhelming because their mental energy is consumed by arithmetic rather than mathematical reasoning.

Jemma Sherwood, author and Senior Lead Practitioner at Ormiston Academies Trust, reminds us that fluency in the four operations – addition, subtraction, multiplication and division – is the foundation of maths understanding (Sherwood, 2018). For resistant learners, building fluency must boost confidence, not anxiety. With older students, it also means respecting their maturity while addressing real gaps. Many carry shame about not knowing times tables, seeing it not as a missing skill but as proof they're 'just not good at maths'. This chapter explores how we can shift the narrative – turning fluency from a source of embarrassment into a path to confidence. It's about supporting students who've missed key foundations, while maintaining their engagement and self-respect throughout.

The cascade effect of missing fluency

Mathematical fluency isn't just about speed – it's about cognitive freedom. When students instantly recall facts like $7 \times 8 = 56$, their working memory is freed up for deeper thinking: spotting patterns, solving problems and understanding concepts. Without that fluency, each basic calculation becomes a multi-step hurdle that blocks higher-level learning.

Take a basic algebra problem like $7x + 8x = 15x$. A fluent student can focus on combining like terms and understanding the structure of the equation. But for someone still unsure whether $7 + 8$ equals 15, the cognitive load shifts entirely. They lose sight of the algebra and get stuck in the arithmetic. Most students don't grasp that x represents an unknown quantity and that this equation is describing 7 lots of something, plus 8 more lots, making 15 in total.

This cascade effect ripples through the curriculum. Students who struggle with multiplication facts often find fractions intimidating, because solving something like $\frac{3}{4} + \frac{2}{3}$ requires confidence with both multiplication and fraction manipulation. Percentage problems become exhausting rather than straightforward: calculating 15% of 80 turns into a multi-step challenge instead of a quick application of a concept.

This kind of avoidance creates a vicious cycle. Over time, it shapes identity – students begin to see themselves as 'not maths people'. But they're not lacking ability; they're missing specific automated skills that can be built with the right support. How many students avoid problems not because they don't understand the concept, but because the *calculation* feels too hard?

Student voice: The hidden impact of fluency gaps

'In the test, I knew how to do the percentage question, but I got stuck on 15% of 80 because I couldn't work out the calculation quickly enough. I ran out of time and felt stupid, even though I understand percentages.'

'I understand what algebra means, but when there are numbers like 6×9 in the equation, I lose track of what I'm doing because I'm concentrating so hard on the maths.'

These experiences reveal the emotional dimension of fluency gaps, too. Students often feel frustrated, not because they lack mathematical understanding, but because missing skills prevent them from showing what they know. Over time, that frustration builds, shaping the mathematical resistance we encounter.

Understanding mathematical fluency

Mathematical fluency is more than quick recall. It's about understanding, flexibility and confidence. For students aiming for Grade 4 and beyond, gaps often remain in the nine foundational areas: addition, subtraction, multiplication, division, fractions, decimals, percentages, scale and ratio. Examiner reports consistently highlight these gaps, even among students working at Grades 5 and 6.

Fluency underpins reasoning and problem solving, as Colin Foster's research shows (Foster, 2019). It allows students to recall facts automatically, apply efficient strategies, switch between methods, recognise patterns and check their work using number sense. This deeper view of fluency moves us away from drill-and-kill approaches that often lead to anxiety. Instead, it promotes understanding alongside automation, building knowledge that transfers to new contexts.

For resistant learners, the key insight is that fluency can be developed at any age. Secondary students and adult learners don't need to be taught like primary children. They need structured, respectful support to build the automated skills that transform their mathematical experience.

The nine essential mathematical skills

These core skills are the foundation of mathematical confidence and competence. Without fluency in them, students struggle to access higher-level thinking. But fluency isn't just about memorising facts – it's about building understanding that lasts.

Let's start with addition and subtraction. These are central to number sense. In primary school, we focus on number bonds, and rightly so. Students need to instantly recall combinations that make 20, like $12 + 8 = 20$ or $13 + 7 = 20$, and understand the related subtraction facts. These basics support mental strategies for larger numbers and free up working memory for algebraic thinking.

Take this example: $12 + 5 + 17 + 28 + 13 + 15$. Some students will go left to right. Others will group cleverly: $(12 + 28) + (5 + 15) + (17 + 13)$. This kind of flexibility comes from fluency built on understanding.

And it matters. A student who struggles with $8 + 7$ will find $18 + 27$ tough. If they can't quickly see that $15 - 7 = 8$, they'll likely struggle with algebra, combining like terms, solving equations and more.

> **Teaching tip: Building addition facts through understanding**
>
> Instead of drilling facts, help students *see* the relationships:
>
> - Doubles: 6 + 6 = 12, so 6 + 7 = 13
> - Near doubles: 8 + 7 = 8 + 8 − 1 = 15
> - Bridging through 10: 7 + 8 = 7 + 3 + 5 = 10 + 5 = 15
>
> These strategies make facts memorable and meaningful.

Multiplication and division facts are equally essential. Students need fluent recall from 1×1 to 12×12, and the matching division facts. But again, fluency grows best through understanding. If a student knows that $6 \times 4 = 4 \times 6$, they've grasped commutativity – and they only need to learn half the facts. Show them how this links to area: a rectangle with sides 6 and 4. Suddenly, multiplication becomes more than a table – it's a concept. Patterns help too (see Classroom Activity).

Finally, place value is arguably the most important fluency skill in secondary maths. Students need to multiply and divide by 10, 100 and 1000 with ease. They should instantly see that 347 = 300 + 40 + 7 and understand how this supports calculation strategies.

Decimal place value is key too. Knowing that 0.12 is *nought point one two*, not *nought point twelve*, shows real understanding. This fluency underpins work with decimals, standard form, estimation and proportional reasoning.

> **Classroom activity: Discovering multiplication patterns**
>
> Instead of drilling times tables, invite students into a space of mathematical discovery. Exploring patterns not only builds fluency – it nurtures curiosity and deeper thinking.
>
> 1 Start with the times 9 pattern, where the digits of each product always sum to 9 (e.g. $9 \times 3 = 27$ and $2 + 7 = 9$).
> 2 Then move to the times 11 pattern for numbers up to 9, where the digit simply repeats (e.g. $11 \times 4 = 44$). These patterns are satisfying to uncover and help students build connections rather than rely on memorisation.

> 3 Encourage students to build unknown facts from known ones. For example, if they know 6 × 6 = 36, they can reason that 6 × 7 = 36 + 6 = 42. This kind of strategic thinking supports automatic recall while reinforcing understanding.
>
> This approach feels like genuine mathematical exploration rather than remedial work. It also maintains student dignity and fosters confidence in those who've struggled with traditional methods.

The remaining essential skills follow the same principle: build fluency through understanding and meaningful practice, not isolated drill.

- Number bonds show how numbers combine to make larger ones, supporting mental calculation and flexibility.
- Fraction equivalence and basic operations help students manipulate and compare quantities with confidence.
- Percentage–decimal–fraction connections allow students to move fluidly between representations, a key skill in real-world maths.
- Estimation and number sense support reasonableness checks and strategic thinking across all topics.

Each of these areas benefits from approaches that make sense to students – methods that connect, rather than confuse. When fluency is built this way, it sticks. And more importantly, it empowers.

> **Hear from the expert: Jemma Sherwood, author and Senior Lead Practitioner at Ormiston Academies Trust**
>
> 'When we first encounter a mathematical idea, we start to build our familiarity with it. What does it mean? Where does it reach? How can I "do" it and how might I "use" it? Once we're familiar with an idea, we can start to build up to fluency, when we can "do" it with ease and can begin to apply it confidently in unexpected situations. Moving from familiarity to fluency needs lots of varied practice and exposure to the idea in different ways. It's a challenge, but well worth it!'

Diagnosing fluency gaps with care

Before building fluency, we need to identify gaps – without causing anxiety, especially for older learners. The key is to frame assessment as support, not a test of what students don't know. Traditional methods like timed tests or public recall often feel punitive and reinforce maths anxiety. Instead, use diagnostic approaches that are calm, respectful and purposeful. When students feel safe and understood, they're more likely to engage honestly. This gives us the insight we need to target support effectively without undermining confidence or progress.

Diagnostic tool: Fluency check (suitable for any age)

To build fluency, we first need to understand where students are starting from. This simple diagnostic activity helps identify gaps in a way that feels safe and constructive for learners of any age.

- Present students with cards showing calculations like 7 + 6, 9 + 8 or 5 + 7. If they respond within three seconds, it suggests fluent recall. Longer responses often indicate reliance on calculation strategies rather than automatic knowledge.
- For multiplication, observe whether students instantly know facts like 6 × 7, 8 × 4 or 9 × 3, or if they rely on counting, repeated addition or other derived methods. These observations offer valuable insight into their fluency development.
- Division connections are especially revealing. After showing 6 × 7 = 42, immediately ask, 'What's 42 ÷ 6?' Fluent students will respond quickly, recognising the inverse relationship. Those still building fluency may need to recalculate or work through the connection step by step.
- Place value can be checked with questions like 'What's 63 × 10?' or 'What's 270 ÷ 10?' These reveal whether students have internalised place value operations or are relying on procedural methods.
- Estimation tasks – such as 19 × 21 – show whether students can use number sense (e.g. recognising this is roughly 20 × 20 = 400) or feel stuck without exact methods.

The most important part of any diagnostic work is the atmosphere. Keep it growth-oriented and supportive. Gaps should be seen as normal and addressable, not as deficits or failures.

Building fluency through understanding and strategy

With older students, fluency development needs to respect their maturity while meeting their learning needs. The most effective approaches focus on mathematical relationships, pattern recognition and strategic thinking – not repetitive drilling, which often increases anxiety without deepening understanding. Visual and conceptual strategies are powerful here.

- Array models help students see 6×4 as a rectangle with 6 rows of 4 objects. This makes the relationship visible and memorable, supporting gradual recall.
- Number lines, horizontal or vertical, for addition and subtraction show efficient jumping strategies, which many students find more intuitive than abstract memorisation.
- Strategic development builds new facts from known ones. A student who knows $5 \times 6 = 30$ can reason that $6 \times 6 = 30 + 6 = 36$, and then $6 \times 7 = 36 + 6 = 42$. This derived-facts approach builds fluency while maintaining mathematical reasoning and offering multiple pathways to the right answer.

Script box: Addressing fluency anxiety

When a student says: 'I'm too old to not know my times tables. I should have learned these years ago.'

- Say this: 'Lots of successful adults have gaps in basic facts – but they're still strong mathematical thinkers. We're going to build your fluency in ways that make sense to you now, using the understanding you've developed as a mature learner.'
- Not this: 'Don't worry, we'll get you caught up quickly – we'll have weekly tests.'
- Follow-up: 'What parts of maths do you feel confident with? Let's build from your strengths and add the fluency that will make everything else easier.'

Creating daily fluency routines that work

Consistent, brief practice is far more effective than cramming when it comes to developing automatic recall. The most successful approaches weave fluency into everyday maths learning, rather than treating it as separate or remedial. This links into the 5Rs curriculum approach from Chapter 3.

A simple five-minute daily routine can make a big difference:

- **Minutes 1–2:** Warm up with previously secure facts to maintain confidence and consolidate learning.
- **Minutes 3–4:** Focus on specific facts or strategies students are currently developing. Use varied formats – written, verbal, visual – to keep engagement high and support different learning preferences.
- **Minute 5:** Apply developing fluency in a meaningful problem-solving context. This final step helps students see the purpose of their practice and connects fluency to real mathematical thinking.

Game-based activities offer a natural, low-pressure way to practise fluency while keeping students engaged. They reduce anxiety and create a sense of enjoyment around maths – especially important for learners who may associate fluency work with past struggles. Number Battle is a simple but effective game: students draw two cards, multiply them, and the highest product wins the round. It provides repeated multiplication practice without feeling like remedial work.

Target Number challenges are another great option. Ask students to find different ways to make a target number – like 24 – using two numbers (e.g. $6 \times 4, 8 \times 3, 12 \times 2$). This builds fluency while encouraging flexibility and creative thinking.

Classroom activity: Fluency stations

Set up rotating stations for 15-minute fluency sessions that offer variety, structure, and meaningful practice:

- Station 1: Card games that require quick calculations in a social, low-pressure setting.
- Station 2: Online fluency apps for individual, self-paced practice.
- Station 3: Pattern exploration and relationship discovery to build understanding alongside automation.
- Station 4: Real-world problems that require fluent calculation in context.

Students rotate through the stations, gaining diversified practice that supports fluency through multiple pathways. This approach avoids the boredom and anxiety often linked to repetitive drilling, while ensuring systematic development of essential skills.

Fluency stations work particularly well because they embed fluency development into everyday maths, rather than presenting it as a remedial fix. This approach helps students feel supported and included, while still addressing genuine learning needs in a structured, purposeful way. They can also be adapted for students with different needs:

For students with dyscalculia:

- Use visual and spatial representations of number relationships.
- Allow calculator access for complex calculations while building basic fact fluency.
- Incorporate colour coding and visual patterns to support memory.
- Use concrete manipulatives when helpful – regardless of age.
- Break fluency development into small, manageable steps with frequent success experiences.

For students with ADHD:

- Integrate movement-based learning (e.g. clapping rhythms, physical arrays).
- Use fidget tools during practice to support focus.
- Keep practice segments short with clear transitions.
- Gamify fluency work with immediate feedback.
- Offer choice in practice methods to support autonomy and engagement.

For students with autism spectrum conditions:

- Provide clear structure and predictable routines.
- Connect fluency practice to special interests where possible.
- Allow processing time without pressure for immediate responses.
- Use visual schedules with clear expectations.
- Recognise that alternative pathways to fluency can be just as valid and effective.

Supporting diverse learners in fluency development reminds us that every student's journey is unique… and so is every teacher's. Just as students may need alternative pathways to build fluency, teachers may also carry their own experiences and uncertainties around basic facts. This brings us to an important and often unspoken part of fluency work: what if you're not fluent yourself?

Confidence builder: Teaching fluency when you're not fluent

It's okay to not feel fluent yourself: your role isn't to be a human calculator, but a guide. Focus on strategies and relationships. Use visual tools, tech and collaborative learning to support both you and your students.

Model problem solving, not just recall. This shows fluency grows through reasoning, not memorisation. Learning alongside students builds trust and shows that maths is a lifelong journey. Your openness can inspire theirs.

The connection between fluency and mathematical identity

Fluency doesn't just improve performance. It transforms how students relate to mathematics. When basic facts become automatic, students can focus their mental energy on deeper thinking. This unlocks success in problem solving, which builds confidence, encourages engagement and creates more opportunities for meaningful practice. Over time, fluency fuels a positive cycle of growth.

For many students, this shift is a turning point. One Year 10 student described how 'algebra suddenly made sense' once multiplication facts became automatic. Without getting stuck on the arithmetic, they could finally focus on the structure and logic of algebra. Another student shared that they used to avoid percentage questions because the calculations took too long. Now, with fluency in place, they can concentrate on what the question is asking rather than battling the numbers.

These moments of clarity reveal the deeper impact of fluency. It's not just about speed, it's about access. Students move from avoidance to engagement, from self-doubt to growing confidence. Fluency helps them see themselves as capable mathematicians, ready to take on challenges with a sense of agency and belief in their ability.

But fluency built on memorisation alone is fragile. It often fails to transfer to new situations or support deeper mathematical thinking. That's why effective fluency development must go hand in hand with number sense – an intuitive grasp of numerical relationships and what makes an answer reasonable.

Students need to be able to estimate and judge whether an answer makes sense. If a student calculates $23 \times 19 = 47$, strong number sense will immediately flag this as unreasonable: it should be close to $20 \times 20 = 400$. This kind of reasonableness checking becomes automatic over time and is essential for building accuracy and confidence. Estimation isn't a side skill, it's something to introduce often, ideally with every calculation attempt.

Encouraging multiple representations helps students see numbers flexibly. For example, 24 can be seen as 6×4, $20 + 4$, 3×8, or $30 - 6$. This flexibility supports both fluency and problem solving by offering multiple pathways to solutions and ways to check work. Open questions like 'If the answer is 120, what might the question be?' invite students to explore this using mini-whiteboards and expand their thinking.

Pattern recognition also plays a key role. Students who notice that odd × odd = odd, even × even = even, or that numbers ending in 5 multiplied by even numbers end in 0, begin to develop shortcuts and insights that transfer across contexts. These patterns strengthen both memory and reasoning.

Supportive assessment

Fluency assessment should focus on individual growth and development rather than comparison to external standards or other students. The goal is documenting progress and identifying next steps, not ranking or categorising students.

Individual progress tracking through fluency portfolios allows students to maintain records of their mathematical fact development, including strategies learned, patterns discovered and applications mastered. Before and after comparisons document students' approaches to calculation at different points, showing growth and development over time.

Strategy interviews prove more valuable than correctness testing. Rather than simply checking whether answers are right, ask students to explain their calculation methods. An open question such as '$18 \times 5 = 90$. How many different ways can you find to make 90?' reveals understanding, identifies effective approaches and highlights areas needing further development.

Error analysis provides crucial diagnostic information. When students make mistakes, explore their thinking to understand whether errors stem from conceptual misunderstanding, procedural confusion or simple recall gaps. This information guides targeted intervention rather than generic remediation. Spoof analysis (see Chapter 11) is also an effective strategic approach. Showing students a question with an answer that someone else has given and asking what mistake have they made reduces anxiety and encourages working with mistakes.

Real-world applications

Students need to see how mathematical fluency supports practical problem solving and career applications. These links help transform abstract skill development into purposeful learning – something students value and are more likely to engage with.

Making these connections explicit helps fluency feel relevant to students' aspirations. In retail and service roles, for example, quick percentage calculations are essential for working out discounts, tips and tax. Mental arithmetic is needed for making change and calculating totals on the spot. In construction and trades, fluency supports rapid measurement conversions, estimating material quantities, and working with proportions, especially when mixing materials or scaling plans. Healthcare careers rely on fluent number sense for dosage calculations, solution ratios and interpreting statistical data. Meanwhile, in business and finance, fluency is key for calculating profit margins and interest rates, and analysing ratios to support informed decision-making.

By showing students how fluency applies beyond the classroom, we help them see it not just as a skill to master but as a tool that opens doors to opportunity, independence and confidence in the world beyond school or college.

Fluency in action

Presenting authentic scenarios from various careers helps students understand that fluent calculation isn't just a classroom skill – it's a tool for solving real problems.

For example, a chef might need to triple a recipe to make it for 12 people instead of 4, requiring proportional reasoning and multiplication fluency. A shop worker calculates a 20% discount on £47.99, using percentage and estimation skills. A mechanic evaluates whether a 15% efficiency increase is significant, drawing on proportional understanding and number sense.

As Paul Wassan, vocational chef tutor, reminds us, 'Some of the things we use in catering, like portioning, timing, temperature control, are maths even if students don't realise it. That's what gives them real-world experience.' By embedding maths into practical, hands-on tasks, we reduce barriers and increase engagement, especially when students are working in areas they've chosen and care about.

Supporting fluency with technology

Technology can be a powerful tool for supporting fluency when it's used with purpose. It should enhance learning, not replace the need for mental mathematical competence. Automatic recall remains essential, and tech should serve as a scaffold, not a substitute.

Well-chosen platforms personalise practice and keep challenge levels appropriate. Adaptive tools adjust difficulty, while pattern apps help students visualise relationships and strengthen memory. Real-world simulators like budgeting or measurement tasks embed fluency in authentic contexts, making practice more meaningful and motivating.

Creating classroom environments that support fluency development

Fluency doesn't grow in isolation; it's shaped by the environment students learn in. Classrooms that naturally encourage practice, while preserving dignity and engagement, create the best conditions for mathematical growth.

Visual supports like multiplication charts, number patterns and fraction equivalences help students make connections without needing to ask. Estimation stations offer quick, informal spaces to test ideas and practise mental maths. Strategy posters give students independent access to efficient methods and ways of thinking. Some educators, like Peps Mccrea, argue that these displays can distract or even demotivate older students who see them as childish (Mccrea, 2020). But the truth is: you know your students. You know what they'll respond to and what they won't.

Celebrating progress, whether through charts, certificates or achievement boards, helps students see their own growth. The focus is on personal development, not comparison.

Routine matters. Daily number talks, 'fact of the day' moments and mental maths warm-ups embed fluency into everyday learning. Tools like Mathsbot's 'Number of the Day' can be used at the start of lessons or during tutor time. These can be tech-based or paper-based, whatever works best for your setting.

And fluency isn't just for maths lessons. When students see it applied in science, geography or design technology, it becomes real. Cross-curricular connections show that fluent thinking travels.

Supporting teacher confidence in fluency instruction

Fluency instruction can feel daunting, especially for teachers unsure of their own recall or concerned about triggering anxiety in students with negative maths experiences. But confidence grows through curiosity, not perfection.

Learning alongside students is powerful. Exploring patterns together builds understanding and models a growth mindset. Online resources can refresh your own fluency, and conversations with colleagues often surface practical strategies. CPD focused on conceptual understanding – not speed – shifts the focus from performance to progress. A teacher might say, 'I remember $7 \times 8 = 56$ because of 5-6-7-8,' or '$3 \times 4 = 12$, which is 1-2-3-4!' These show fluency is about meaningful connections, not just memory.

Most importantly: facilitating learning isn't about demonstrating personal fluency. Your role is to create conditions for success through strategy, structure and support. When students see you model thoughtful approaches and celebrate effort, they learn fluency is something they can build too.

Long-term fluency development

Fluency is a journey, not a one-time goal. It evolves as students move through education. What matters in Year 7 differs from Year 11, and shifts again in post-16 and adult learning. Understanding this progression helps teachers set realistic, purposeful expectations.

In Years 10–11, fluency goes beyond times tables. Students need automatic recall of multiplication and division facts, confident percentage calculations (10%, 25%, 50%, 75%) and ease with converting between fractions, decimals and percentages. These skills underpin GCSE success and wider numeracy.

In post-16 and adult learning, fluency includes algebraic manipulation, statistical literacy and confident data interpretation. Students also develop fluency with tools (ruler, protractor, compass, calculator) while relying on mental strategies to check and apply results. Maths becomes a tool for real-world thinking, supporting decision-making, problem solving and communication in career-specific contexts.

Adapting to your setting

- **GCSE classrooms:** Integrate fluency development across the nine basic skills into regular lessons through warm-up activities, problem-solving contexts and cross-curricular applications. This helps make skill development feel natural and embedded, rather than remedial.
- **Resit students:** Address fluency gaps with sensitivity, focusing on immediate, practical benefits. Use adult-appropriate contexts and recognise the mathematical thinking students already bring, while building the automated skills they may have missed.
- **Vocational support contexts:** Connect fluency directly to trade and career-specific applications, showing how automatic calculation supports professional competence and workplace efficiency.
- **One-to-one intervention:** Create highly personalised fluency plans based on individual gaps, learning preferences and specific goals. Use instructional flexibility to meet particular needs while maintaining motivation and engagement.
- **SEND:** Adapt fluency development to individual learning differences, maintaining high expectations and celebrating diverse forms of mathematical competence and achievement.

Key research points

- Dylan Wiliam: Cognitive Load Theory
  - Key takeaway: Working memory has limited capacity; automatic recall frees up space for deeper thinking.
  - Use it: Prioritise fluency as foundational work that enables – not replaces – conceptual understanding and problem solving.
- US Department of Education: National Mathematics Advisory Panel
  - Key takeaway: Fluency with basic facts is essential for success in complex mathematics across the curriculum.
  - Use it: Systematically address fluency gaps rather than assuming they'll close through general exposure.
- AQA Basic Skills Questions, Teacher Rationale and Question Sets
  - Key takeaway: Fluency in the nine basics of maths is key to success.
  - Use it: Read the teacher rationale and try out the three questions sets with students.

Reflection questions

- How do I currently assess and address mathematical fluency gaps in my students without creating anxiety or embarrassment?
- Which basic mathematical skills are most crucial for my students' current learning and future mathematical success?
- How can I develop fluency approaches that build confidence rather than create anxiety, especially for students who've experienced mathematical trauma?
- What environmental and instructional supports could I provide to encourage ongoing fluency development while maintaining student dignity?

Next steps

1. Start by doing a fluency audit using age-appropriate diagnostic tools that focus on understanding student needs, rather than highlighting deficits. This helps identify where support is most needed and ensures interventions are targeted and respectful.
2. Gather a range of strategy resources (activities, routines and tools) that suit your students and your teaching context.
3. Create systems for monitoring progress that track individual growth while maintaining privacy and dignity.
4. Plan integration approaches that embed fluency practice into regular lessons. Use meaningful contexts and practical applications to make fluency feel like a natural part of maths learning.

Chapter 5

Fundamental Maths Knowledge

Building secure foundations for mathematical confidence

'How many centimetres are in a metre?' It's a simple question, but ask it in class and you'll see a range of reactions. Some students freeze. Others guess: 'Is it 10? 100? 1000?' A few glance around, hoping someone else will jump in first.

These responses tell us more than who knows the answer. They reveal students who've come to see maths as a series of facts they're expected to know, but don't. For learners who already feel resistant, every 'I should know this but I don't' moment chips away at their confidence.

Behind those uncertain answers are often complex stories. Some students have missed key lessons due to illness, family moves or caring responsibilities. Others understand the maths but struggle with the vocabulary. Some have faced financial stress or disrupted schooling. Many feel embarrassed about gaps they had no control over.

It's easy to assume that basic facts like conversions, properties of shape and time are secure by secondary school, college or FE. But for many students, these ideas feel fuzzy rather than firm. They might guess well enough to get by, but they don't feel confident. Often, they've had limited practice, or they see these facts as random rules rather than connected ideas. When knowledge feels shaky, anxiety creeps in.

To close fluency gaps, we first need to understand why knowledge hasn't stuck. Maths is a web of ideas: if a student doesn't know there are 100 cm in a metre, calculating area becomes confusing. These gaps create a domino effect. Each topic builds on the last, so missing foundations can erode confidence. This has worsened post-pandemic, with missed consolidation and fewer everyday experiences like handling cash or reading analogue clocks.

Exams reflect the importance of basics. At Foundation Tier GCSE, 50 per cent of marks are for recall and routine procedures; at Higher Tier, it's 40 per cent. These skills appear throughout the paper – from simple questions to complex problems. But it's not just about exams. In real life, fluency matters. Bricklayers, for example, measure in millimetres and metres, often skipping centimetres. They need to switch units quickly and accurately.

The emotional dimension of knowledge gaps

Student voice: When fundamental knowledge feels unsafe

Here's how your students might describe their experience:

- 'I always forget how many centimetres in a metre… I've been taught it loads of times but it just doesn't stick.'
- 'Is a right angle 90 degrees or 180? I can never remember.'
- 'Why do we need to know all these random facts when we can just look them up?'
- 'Every time I try to convert units, I get confused whether to multiply or divide.'

The first statement might point to working memory challenges, anxiety or simply not enough meaningful practice. Confusion about right angles often means students haven't connected abstract numbers to visual understanding. When they ask why they need to memorise facts, they're often unsure when quick recall is useful and when it's okay to use tools. And conversion confusion usually means they've learned steps without grasping the concept. Many students struggle with foundational ideas like money, measurement, time and place value. These gaps shake their confidence and make them reluctant to engage.

Different pathways to secure knowledge

To close these gaps, we need to design learning that works for everyone, including our students with additional needs. This shouldn't be an add-on, but a starting point.

Students with dyscalculia may find it hard to remember facts. Those with ADHD might struggle to focus during recall activities. Students on the autism spectrum often benefit from clear patterns and predictable routines. These aren't barriers – they're opportunities to rethink how we teach. Dr Steve Chinn reminds us that 'any work that is not constantly refreshed is often lost' (Chinn, 2012). That's true for students with diagnosed learning differences, and also for those whose education has been disrupted by trauma, instability or other challenges.

So what helps? Here are a few pointers:

- emphasising patterns over memorisation
- using hands-on activities and visual aids
- building procedural understanding alongside factual recall
- offering repeated practice for some, and ongoing support for others.

There's no one-size-fits-all approach – and that's okay. What matters is that every student feels maths is something they *can* do, not something they're expected to already know.

Working with memory differences

Supporting students who struggle with fact retention isn't about pushing them to memorise more, it's about helping them feel secure in their mathematical thinking. Some learners will always need reference tools, and that's perfectly fine. What matters is that they can reason, problem-solve and make sense of the maths in front of them.

One way to build confidence is by using visual memory aids (e.g. charts, diagrams and patterns) that students can picture and return to. Linking new facts to familiar visuals helps make abstract ideas more concrete. For many students, especially those with additional needs, concrete–pictorial–abstract routines offer a reliable way in. A metre stick, a pie chart, a set of Dienes blocks aren't just props; they're bridges to understanding. I have curated a very popular padlet of mathematical hooks which you may find useful (see Further Reading and Resources).

It also helps to build on what students already know. Etymology, the origin of words, can be a surprisingly powerful tool here. When we explain that 'cent', which originates from 'centum', means 100 (like cents in a dollar or a century of years) it gives students a hook to hang new knowledge on. These connections aren't just clever; they're memorable and build upon what students already know.

Multi-sensory approaches are another key strategy. Some students need to *feel* the maths – literally. Manipulating objects, writing things out or saying them out loud can all help embed understanding. And when students show partial knowledge, it's worth celebrating. If they grasp the relationship but can't recall the number, say,

'You understand the connection and that's the important part.' Ultimately, our goal isn't just to improve memory, it's to build mathematical resilience. Students can succeed in maths even if they rely on supports for basic facts. What matters is that they feel capable, curious and included.

Essential knowledge that builds confidence

Of course, confidence alone isn't enough, we also need to be strategic. Instead of overwhelming students with every measurement fact they might encounter, focus on the essentials: length conversions, mass relationships, capacity measures, time calculations and angle facts. These are the building blocks of success at GCSE level.

For students with memory difficulties, patterns are powerful. Most measurements – length, weight, volume – follow a base-10 system: 10s, 100s, 1000s. Time is the exception, which makes it stand out. Teaching this simple structure helps reduce cognitive load and gives students a framework they can rely on. It's not about memorising isolated facts – it's about seeing how they fit together.

This pattern-based approach is especially helpful for students who struggle with rote learning. It shifts the focus from recall to understanding, and that shift can make all the difference.

Teaching tip: Boosting memory with etymology

Maths vocabulary can be tricky but it doesn't have to be dry. By linking new terms to familiar words, we make them stickier and more meaningful. Try these in class:

- **Measurement conversions:**

    'There are 100 cents in a dollar and 100 centimetres in a metre. Same idea!' 'A millennium is 1000 years. So, how many millimetres in a metre? That's right – 1000!'

- **Geometric vocabulary:**

    'A tricycle has three wheels, just like a triangle has three sides.' 'Quadruplets means four babies. A quadrilateral has four sides.'

- **Operations:**

    'Addition comes from 'ad' meaning 'to': we're adding *to* a number.' 'Subtraction means 'taking away'; 'sub' means under or away from.'

Use these connections often. Write them on the board, build displays and refer back to them when students forget. These links help students anchor new knowledge in what they already understand and they often find them surprisingly fun. That shift from frustration to curiosity is a win in itself.

Of course, even with clever connections, students will still ask: 'Why do I need to know this?' And it's a fair question. In a world of smartphones and instant answers, memorising facts can feel unnecessary.

Script box: Answering 'Why do we need this?'

Here's how to respond in a way that builds trust and understanding:

- Say this: 'Great question! Professionals often need to recall facts quickly to do their jobs well and safely. A carpenter who constantly looks up conversions might make mistakes and lose clients. These facts are like tools – experts rely on them without stopping to think.'
- Not this: 'Because it's on the exam.'
- Follow-up: 'Let's look at some real-life examples of how these facts are used in different careers – and what happens when they're missing.'

This kind of conversation helps students see maths as practical, not just academic. But we also need to go further – beyond explanation, into experience. Use real objects. Let students *see* and *touch* the relationships. Count the centimetres on a metre stick together. Pour water into measuring jugs and compare millilitres to litres. These moments make maths tangible. They turn abstract ideas into shared discoveries. And that's the heart of it. When students feel involved – when they're not just told but invited to explore – they begin to trust their own thinking. They stop seeing maths as something mysterious and start seeing it as something they can do.

Classroom dialogue: Supporting different learning needs

Teacher: 'Today we're working with angle measurements. I know some of you might find it tricky to remember all the angle facts.'

Student: 'I'm always stuck on whether a triangle has 180 or 360 degrees.'

Teacher: 'That's totally okay! Instead of just trying to memorise it, let's make a physical model together. Here's a triangle I've cut out from paper. If we cut off the angles and rearrange them, what do you think will happen?'

Student: *(playing with the angles)* 'Oh, they make a straight line!'

Teacher: 'Exactly! And how many degrees are on a straight line?'
Student: '180 degrees!'
Teacher: 'Spot on. So, whenever you need to remember the angles in a triangle, just picture rearranging it into a straight line.'

This isn't a formal proof, of course, but it's a powerful demonstration. It helps students *see* the relationship, not just hear it. And that's the kind of experience that sticks.

Practical approaches for immediate implementation

Concrete experiences like this are a brilliant way to build understanding. But for lasting change, they need to be part of a wider plan – a structured, consistent approach that helps students develop and retain essential knowledge over time.

1 **Identify prerequisite knowledge**: Before introducing a new topic, take a moment to jot down the key facts students need to access it confidently. For area calculations, they'll need to understand length conversions and multiplication facts. For bearings, they'll need angle facts and compass directions. A simple checklist for each topic can make planning more focused and responsive.

2 **Use entry tickets as diagnostic tools**: Start lessons with two or three quick questions to check what students already know, e.g.:
   - 'How many centimetres are in a metre?'
   - 'What's the formula for the area of a rectangle?'
   - 'What units do we use to measure area?'

   This takes just a couple of minutes but gives you a clear picture of where your class is starting from.

3 **Address gaps immediately**: If those entry tickets show gaps, spend five minutes reinforcing the basics before moving on. Use hands-on demonstrations or visual prompts rather than repeating facts verbally. This keeps the lesson inclusive and ensures no one gets left behind.

By embedding these steps into your routine, you make foundational knowledge part of everyday teaching instead of an occasional intervention. It becomes manageable, consistent and something students come to expect and value.

> **Teaching tip: Make learning fun with spaced practice**
>
> Spaced practice is a gentle but powerful way to help facts stick. Here's a simple plan to follow:
>
> - **Week 1:** Introduce five key facts. Use hands-on demos, word associations or visual patterns. Spend just three minutes at the start of each lesson practising them together.
> - **Week 2:** Add five new facts, while still reviewing the first five. Now you're practising ten facts daily.
> - **Week 3:** Add another five. Review all fifteen, but rotate the Week 1 facts every other day to keep things fresh.
> - **Week 4:** Continue adding new facts. Move well-known ones to weekly reviews, and keep tricky ones in daily practice.
>
> This steady rhythm helps students build confidence gradually. They see their knowledge grow, and that sense of progress is incredibly motivating.

For extra support, try Corbettmaths 5-a-day (see Further Reading and Resources). It's a brilliant resource with question sets starting from the numeracy level, focused on core facts. Students can self-assess and bring only the tricky ones to you – ideal for busy classrooms. Another great tool is Mathsbot (see Further Reading and Resources), created by Jonny Hall. It offers structured starters and retrieval practice that's both varied and systematic. These resources help students embed learning without getting bored or overwhelmed.

> **Hear from the expert: John Corbett, Creator of Corbettmaths.com**
>
> 'One of the biggest challenges I faced as a teacher was to ensure my students were able to confidently recall previously covered material. My solution was to develop the 5-a-day, which gave students the opportunity to use a "Little and Often" approach to promote retention.'

Mistakes as opportunities

Even with the best tools and strategies, mistakes will happen – and that's okay. In fact, they're valuable. Errors show us how students are thinking, where they're stuck, and what support they need next. Instead of seeing mistakes as setbacks, treat them as stepping stones. They're part of the learning journey, and when students feel safe to get things wrong, they're far more likely to take risks, ask questions and grow.

Helping students avoid common errors

It's common for students to mix up their conversions, like when they try to change 3.5 metres into centimetres by dividing by 100. If they end up with 0.035 cm, it shows they might be confused about whether to multiply or divide. This kind of mistake shows us they've grasped part of the idea (that 100 is involved) but are unsure about the direction.

Here's a step-by-step way to support them:

1 **Understand their thinking:** Ask, 'Can you share your thinking with me? Why did you choose to divide?' Often, they'll say something like, 'Because you use 100 to convert,' which shows they're on the right track – they just need help with the process.

2 **Use the size check:** Prompt them: 'Is 3.5 metres bigger or smaller than 1 metre?' (It's bigger!) Then ask, 'If we're converting to centimetres, should the number get bigger or smaller?' This helps them realise that multiplying makes more sense.

3 **Teach a simple rule:** Share this decision rule: 'When converting from larger units to smaller units, we multiply – because we end up with more of the smaller unit. When going from smaller to larger, we divide – because we have fewer of the larger unit.'

4 **Practice with visual support:** Use place value charts, conversion ladders or ratio tables to show how the decimal point shifts when converting. These visuals help make the process clearer and more memorable.

By unpacking the thinking behind mistakes, we offer meaningful support, not just correction. When students understand *why* they got something wrong, they're far more likely to get it right next time.

Confidence builder: For teachers less confident with fundamental facts

If you're not completely secure with these facts yourself, you're not alone – and you're not failing. Here are some gentle ways to build your confidence:

- **Create your own reference sheet.** Jot down key conversions and keep them handy. It's absolutely fine to double-check facts – students appreciate your honesty.
- **Practice etymology connections.** Understanding where terms come from helps you remember them and gives you great content to share with students.
- **Use the same resources as students.** Try Corbettmaths 5-a-day yourself. It's a great way to boost your confidence alongside your learners. There are five levels of the resource, from numeracy to Higher Plus.
- **Focus on understanding over memorisation.** When you understand *why* conversions work, you're less likely to make mistakes – and are better equipped to support others.
- **Be honest with students.** Saying, 'Let me double-check this,' models good mathematical habits. It shows that checking is part of the process, not a weakness.

When you feel good about the basics, you can focus on supporting your students with clarity and confidence.

The Forgetting Curve

One of the biggest challenges students face is forgetting what they've learned. The Ebbinghaus Forgetting Curve helps us understand why this happens and what to do about it. Developed in the 19th century, it shows how quickly memory fades without reinforcement:

- up to 80 per cent of new learning can be forgotten within a week
- the steepest drop happens in the first 24 hours
- just one timely revision can help students retain up to 50 per cent more after a month.

Spaced repetition (reviewing material at increasing intervals) is the most effective way to strengthen memory. When students understand that forgetting is normal, and that there are strategies to help, they become active participants in their learning rather than passive recipients. This approach also helps reduce test anxiety and builds more confident, independent learners.

Creating fun and effective retrieval practice

> **Classroom activity: Memory connections**
>
> Start by asking students to share nursery rhymes or song lyrics they know by heart. Then ask: 'How did you learn these?' Try to elicit the idea that they heard them repeatedly over time, not all at once.
>
> Now connect this to maths. Just like those rhymes, maths facts stick better with regular, gentle practice than with cramming. Set up a routine: five minutes a day reviewing key facts. For students who find nursery rhymes childish, use sports stats, favourite songs or other long-term knowledge.

Script box: Addressing fundamental facts positively

This framing helps students feel supported, not tested. It turns facts into tools for thinking, not hurdles to clear:

- Say this: 'We're looking at area calculations today. First, who can tell me how many millimetres are in a centimetre? These facts are building blocks for everything we'll do.'
- Not this: 'Convert 1.2 metres into centimetres.'
- Follow-up: 'Let's think about word connections. Did you know "century" means 100 years? A centipede has 100 legs! "Cent" means 100 in many languages; that's why there are 100 centimetres in a metre. It shows the relationship between the words "centi" and "metre".'

Building on this positive framing, create reference materials that everyone can use independently. Instead of thinking of them as 'cheating' or giving up, view them as supportive tools that help us think mathematically.

Building systematic knowledge organisers

The best materials have a clear structure with helpful scaffolding. AccessMaths has devised a fantastic way to use pentagon problems that break down complex challenges into five simple skills, giving every student a great starting point while encouraging more advanced thinking (see Further Reading and Resources). The same principle works for our knowledge organisers; we want to create tools that meet students where they are now while guiding them toward even greater progress. Here's how to make effective knowledge organisers:

1. **Focus on essential facts.** Keep it simple. Include only what's needed for the topic at hand.
2. **Use visual organisation.** Group related facts and use colour, boxes or symbols to show connections.
3. **Include worked examples.** Show how the facts apply in real contexts – especially with diagrams.
4. **Add memory aids.** Use etymology and visual patterns to make learning stick.
5. **Make it quizzable.** Design organisers so students can cover sections and quiz themselves – like flashcards.

Nicola Whiston's award-winning knowledge organisers are a brilliant example of how structure and clarity can support independence (Young, n.d.). By combining core facts, worked examples and key mathematical terms, her approach gives students a clear starting point while encouraging deeper thinking. These tools aren't just practical – they're empowering.

To make the most of organisers like these, it helps to think carefully about what we include. Nathan Burns, a metacognition expert, reminds us that less is often more (Burns, 2021). When we curate only the most relevant information and present it clearly, we reduce cognitive load and make learning more accessible. Vocabulary is a great place to start. Abstract terms can feel intimidating, but graphic organisers like Frayer Models (see Further Reading and Resources) help break them down. These tools guide students to explore definitions, characteristics, examples and non-examples, making complex ideas more concrete and easier to remember.

When students can access information confidently (even if they haven't memorised it) they begin to feel more capable. That sense of security is what builds mathematical resilience. It's not just about knowing the answer, it's about knowing how to find it, understand it and use it.

Building confidence

These reference tools are just one part of the puzzle. We also need to create classroom environments where discussing and checking fundamental knowledge feels natural and supportive. Here's an example of how to check prerequisite knowledge in a way that feels collaborative and empowering:

Classroom dialogue: Threshold concepts in practice

Teacher: 'Today we're exploring angles in parallel lines. Let's start by refreshing our memories. What do we already know about angles?'
Student A: 'There are 180° in a triangle!'
Teacher: 'Excellent. Can you name the different types of triangles?'
Student A: 'Equilateral, isosceles, right-angled... and scalene.'
Teacher: 'Great. Now, where else do we find 180°?'
Student B: 'On a straight line?'
Teacher: 'Perfect. And what about 90°?'
Student C: 'That's a right angle!'

This kind of dialogue builds on what students know, connects it to new learning, and shows them they're ready for the challenge ahead. As each response is given, draw a diagram to support it – and encourage students to do the same. Suggest they create flashcards for any facts they're unsure about.

When we treat recall as a shared experience, it becomes less about pressure and more about progress. Students support each other, and you provide the structure that makes the knowledge meaningful and accessible. It's also amazing how often students discover they know more than they thought. That moment of recognition – 'I *do* know this!' – can be a real confidence boost. It's our job to help them turn that spark into something solid: knowledge that's easy to access, connected to new ideas and ready to support deeper learning. When students feel secure in their foundational understanding, they're far more willing to take on the tougher challenges ahead.

Adapting to your setting

- **GCSE classrooms:** Structure is everything. One-page fact sheets for each topic can make a big difference. Before starting a new unit, identify the key knowledge students need and provide a summary they can use for reference and self-testing. This helps reduce anxiety and gives them a clear sense of what's expected.
- **Resit students:** Confidence is often fragile. Begin each session by celebrating what they *do* know. Use quick diagnostic activities to uncover gaps, then address those gaps directly – without assuming they're starting from scratch. This approach helps rebuild trust in their own ability.

- **Vocational support contexts:** Relevance is key. Connect mathematical facts to real-world applications. For example, show bricklayers how accurate measurement conversions affect safety and precision, or help catering students understand ratios by scaling recipes. When students see the link between maths and their future careers, engagement grows.
- **One-to-one interventions:** Personalisation matters – create tailored fact cards that target specific gaps and use the student's interests to make connections stick. If they love football, use match stats or pitch dimensions to explore number facts. These small adjustments can make learning feel more meaningful.
- **Students with memory difficulties:** Make use of pattern-based learning. Instead of focusing on isolated facts, help students spot relationships and use permanent reference tools. Explain that using these supports isn't a shortcut – it's a valid and intelligent way to do maths.
- **Students with disrupted education:** Clarity and compassion go hand in hand – teach missed concepts without shame or assumptions. Use real-life examples that feel age-appropriate, rather than reverting to primary school methods. This helps students feel respected and capable, even when revisiting foundational ideas.

Key research points

- Ebbinghaus Forgetting Curve
    - Key takeaway: Without reinforcement memory fades.
    - Use it: Explore and apply the concept of spaced practice.
- Using Knowledge Organisers
    - Key takeaway: A concise collection of pertinent facts, concepts, methods and vocabulary.
    - Use it: Download existing resources or co-create new knowledge organisers with your students. Use them as appropriate to your students.
- Professor Steve Chinn: *The Trouble with Maths – A Practical Guide in Helping Learners with Numeracy Difficulties*
    - Key takeaway: Any work that isn't constantly refreshed is often lost.
    - Use it: Read and digest the ideas and implement with learners, especially those with additional needs.

Reflection questions

- How do you currently uncover fundamental knowledge gaps in your students' understanding?
- Which students could benefit from the memory support strategies mentioned?
- What methods can you use for retrieval practice? How can you adjust these methods for your teaching?

Next steps

1. Review one topic: Choose a topic you will teach soon and list the basic, fundamental facts students need to know. Create a checklist of prerequisites.
2. Use entry tickets: Start each lesson with 2–3 quick questions to check students' understanding before introducing new material.
3. Start daily practice: Dedicate five minutes each day to practice fundamental facts using spaced retrieval. Use Corbettmaths 5-a-day or make your own question sets.
4. Create reference tools: Make one-page knowledge organisers for the most difficult topics, including visual aids and memory tips.

Chapter 6
Mathematical Methods

Building mathematical toolkits for teachers and students alike

When a student says 'I can't do multiplication' after years of struggling with the standard method, resistance has solidified into a fixed belief that they 'can't do maths'. Most resistant learners have repeatedly failed with one method and consequently believe they're just bad at the whole subject. But what if their problem isn't mathematical ability, it's mathematical method?

> **Student voice**
>
> 'Why has no one ever shown me this method? I always thought I was rubbish at maths until you showed me a different way to multiply using the grid method. I can do it like that!'
>
> 'I've failed GCSE maths three times and I'm 19. When my teacher showed me the Vedic method, I actually got the right answer without having a panic attack because I only had to count. For the first time, maths didn't make me want to cry.'

This chapter breaks down one of biggest myths about mathematics: that there's only one 'right' way to do maths. For students in all contexts, exploring different methods can be a game changer after feeling stuck with traditional approaches. When students find various ways to reach the same answer, it opens up a world of possibilities instead of limitations. Sometimes it is enough to say to the student, 'I don't think you've learned it like that... Have you seen this method?'

The strategies shared here connect perfectly with the 5Rs curriculum (see Chapter 12) approach.

Throughout history, people from all over the world have developed unique ways to calculate and understand numbers. This variety gives us a wonderful toolbox of methods to help every student succeed.

The journey from feeling stuck to becoming confident in maths often starts with a special moment: when students realise that there are many different ways to approach maths. They can find paths that match how they think rather than being pushed into strict rules that don't resonate with them.

Why alternative methods work

Alternative methods can really change the game when it comes to maths learning. They provide new strategies for students who may have faced challenges in the past. By recognising that everyone learns differently, these methods help build confidence and demonstrate that maths can be flexible and adaptable. For those who may have resisted maths in the past, this flexibility is crucial for reshaping how they view their mathematical abilities. Sometimes you'll hear 'I can do it like that… How does that work?'

Reducing maths anxiety through method choice

Research from National Numeracy tells us that about 36 per cent of 15–24 year-olds in the UK experience maths anxiety, often as a result of feeling stuck in traditional teaching methods (National Numeracy, 2019a). Offering alternative calculation techniques helps tackle this anxiety by:

- removing the emotional baggage associated with 'failed' methods
- providing visual and hands-on options for different approaches
- avoiding anxiety-inducing methods like 'carrying' or 'borrowing'
- creating positive experiences that challenge feelings of helplessness.
- showing that there are many ways to approach maths, not just one.

For students, the choice of methods can be a breath of fresh air: 'This isn't the method I used before, so maybe I can succeed this time!' By presenting different approaches, we emphasise that there isn't just one 'right' way to solve a problem and help deepen their understanding of concepts. Remember, any method that gets the right answer deserves appreciation! The aim is to add to our students' mathematical toolbox, giving them the freedom to choose techniques that work for them. This sense of choice and flexibility is essential for building resilience.

Before we move on, take a moment to think about whether your preferred calculation methods work for *all* of your students. If you're honest, they probably don't. Studies show that offering a few alternative methods gives students a sense of choice without overwhelming them (Patall et al., 2008). However, successfully implementing these methods goes beyond just showcasing different techniques.

Building confidence through choice and flexibility: multiplication

Let's take a closer look at this calculation: 23 × 42. Instead of relying solely on the traditional column method, we're going to explore a few different approaches, where each one offers something unique to suit different learners.

Method 1: Traditional column algorithm

This method works well for students who have strong recall of times tables and can manage several steps in their working memory. It's also a good fit for learners who are confident with place value and find it easy to line numbers up correctly.

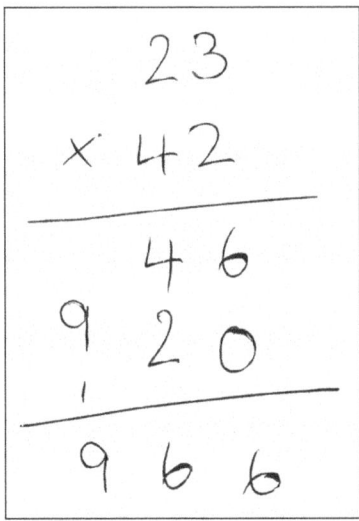

Figure 6.1 Traditional column multiplication diagram showing 23 × 42 = 966

Method 2: The grid method

Cognitive load theory says that our working memory can only manage a limited amount of information at once. While the traditional column method works well for many, it can feel overwhelming for students who find 'carrying' confusing or stressful. That's where the grid method comes in. It's particularly helpful for learners who struggle with place value or need more scaffolding to access the calculation.

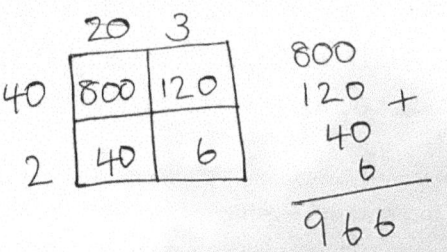

Figure 6.2 Grid method diagram showing 23 × 42 broken into sections.

This approach breaks the multiplication into clear, visible parts:

20 × 40 = 800
20 × 2 = 40
3 × 40 = 120
3 × 2 = 6

Add them together and you get 966, but more importantly, students can *see* how each part contributes to the whole. The visual layout makes place value explicit and removes the pressure of holding too much in working memory. For students with dyscalculia or memory difficulties, this structure offers essential support. It builds understanding alongside calculation skills and lays a strong foundation for future learning, especially when moving into algebra or more abstract concepts.

Method 3: The partial products method

This method is very similar to the grid approach, but without the visual layout. It's a great option for students who benefit from seeing place value clearly but prefer working with numbers in a more linear format. Here's how it works:

23 × 42 = (20 × 40) + (20 × 2) + (3 × 40) + (3 × 2) = 800 + 40 + 120 + 6 = 966

By breaking the calculation into smaller, meaningful parts, this method removes the stress of carrying and makes the maths feel more manageable. It's especially helpful for learners who are developing their understanding of place value or who find multi-step processes overwhelming.

It also supports students who are learning English, as it reduces the language load while keeping the mathematical structure strong. The clear breakdown helps everyone see *why* the answer makes sense – not just *what* the answer is.

Method 4: Napier's bones/the lattice method

This method is helpful for students who find place value or carrying (exchanging) difficult, or who benefit from extra scaffolding. It can also be a more efficient option for those who are confident with the traditional method but prefer something quicker or more visual.

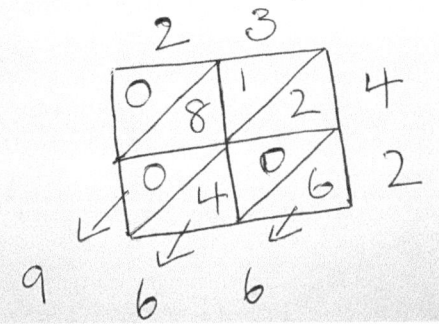

Figure 6.3 The three-step Napier's bones method showing lattice multiplication.

Originally developed by Scottish mathematician John Napier in the 1600s using rods made of bone, wood or ivory, this technique allows students to carry out calculations in a hands-on, structured way, originally without needing to memorise multiplication facts. It's a brilliant tool for anyone who needs a little extra support, and a great reminder that maths has always been full of creative solutions.

What makes this approach so powerful is its flexibility. There's no need to know place value and the relative size of the numbers involved. There's no single starting point, which can be particularly valuable for neurodivergent learners who thrive when given choice and control over how they work. It's a method that adapts to the learner, rather than forcing the learner to adapt to the method.

Method 5: Vedic method

This method is a great fit for students who enjoy spotting patterns and working through systematic steps. It's also helpful for learners who find number formation challenging or feel anxious when faced with traditional calculation methods. It relies purely on the ability to count intersections – no times tables knowledge required.

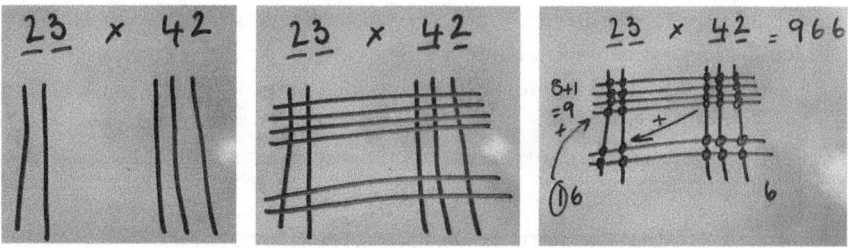

Figure 6.4 The three-step Vedic method diagram showing line intersection counting.

According to Professor Chinn's research, the Vedic method can be a game changer for students with working memory difficulties because instead of relying on memorised multiplication facts, it uses a visual approach (counting intersections) to reach the answer (Chinn, 2019). This makes it a low-stress, highly accessible option for students who feel overwhelmed by more conventional methods.

Originally developed in ancient India and later popularised through Vedic mathematics, this technique offers a calm, structured way into multiplication. It's not just about getting the right answer – it's about helping students feel in control of the process. It is also important to recognise and celebrate cultural difference. Some students who had learned the method elsewhere might tell you that they didn't think they were allowed to use it.

And that sense of control is exactly what many learners need – especially those who've come to believe they're 'just bad at maths'. When we introduce method choice in the classroom, it can be a turning point.

Classroom dialogue: Method introduction

Student: 'I'm rubbish at multiplication. I always mess up the carrying.'

Teacher: 'No worries! Let's explore some different ways to multiply and see what feels right for you. Here are three approaches – take a look and tell me which one you like best.'

Student: 'The grid one looks like something I can actually follow.'

Teacher: 'Perfect! That's your method. And remember, during the exam, you can use whichever method helps you get to the right answer.'

This kind of conversation highlights an important principle: we're not here to force a single method, we're here to help students discover what works best for them. Offering reassurance about the exam helps ease anxiety and empowers learners to make confident choices. It shows them that they're in control and that's the first step towards believing they can do maths.

> **Teaching tip: Building estimation habits**
>
> Before diving into a calculation, try asking students to make a quick estimate first. You might say something like: 'What do you think the rough size of this answer will be? Will it be in the tens, hundreds or thousands?'
>
> For example, with a question like 23 × 42, a student might think: 'Well, 20 × 40 is 800,' which gives them a solid starting point and helps set a realistic expectation.
>
> This simple habit does more than just support accuracy – it builds confidence. When students estimate first, they're more likely to spot errors, feel reassured when their final answer makes sense, and develop a stronger sense of number intuition over time. It's a small shift that can make a big difference in how they approach maths.

Alternative approaches to subtraction

Subtraction can be a real sticking point for many students, especially when it comes to the idea of borrowing, carrying or, as it is now referred to in primary, exchanging. For students with working memory challenges or dyscalculia, this concept feels confusing. But with the right approach, we can help make subtraction clearer and more manageable.

Method 1: Traditional column algorithm

This method works well for students who have a secure understanding of place value and can keep track of multiple steps in their working memory.

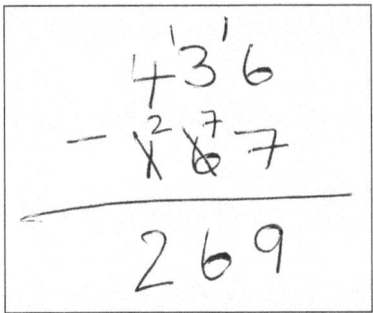

Figure 6.5 The traditional subtraction method, showing 436 − 167 with borrowing.

That said, many learners find the idea of borrowing tricky. For example, when we say 'you can't subtract 7 from 6, so you borrow 10 from the next column,' it can sound a bit misleading to logical thinkers. It's a small detail, but it causes confusion. What are we really borrowing? Where does the 10 come from? These questions matter, and they deserve clear, thoughtful answers.

By recognising where students get stuck, we can begin to offer alternative methods that feel more intuitive and less stressful, especially for those who need a bit more scaffolding to feel confident.

Method 2: Alternative column method using negative numbers

This is a great option for students who are comfortable working with negative numbers and have a secure understanding of place value. Instead of worrying about borrowing, we simply work with the values as they are, even if they're negative.

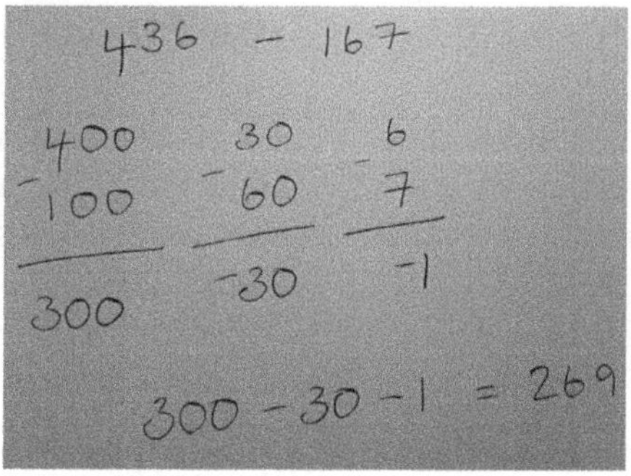

Figure 6.6 Subtraction using negative numbers — 400 – 100 = 300; 30 – 60 = –30; 6 – 7 = –1.

Here's how it works:

$$6 \text{ minus } 7 = -1$$
$$30 \text{ minus } 60 = -30$$
$$400 \text{ minus } 100 = 300$$

Then we combine the parts: 300 – 30 – 1 = 269

This approach removes the stress of borrowing and offers a clear, logical pathway through the calculation. It's particularly helpful for students who question mathematical 'rules' that feel arbitrary or confusing. By reinforcing their understanding of negative numbers, we also build confidence in a concept that often feels intimidating and show that there's more than one way to work things out.

Method 3: Subtraction using rounding

This method is ideal for students who are comfortable with rounding and want to avoid the stress of borrowing or subtracting into negatives.

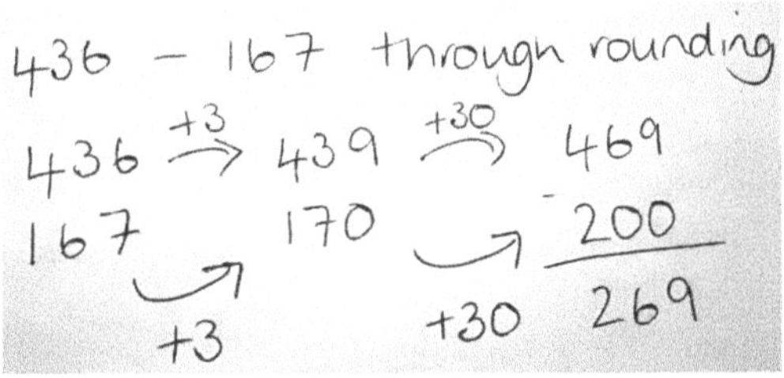

Figure 6.7 Subtraction using rounding.

Instead of working through each digit and worrying about exchanging 1 for 10, students round both numbers by the same amount, to make the subtraction easier while keeping the result the same. This helps them stay focused on the overall size of the numbers and reduces the cognitive load that often comes with traditional subtraction.

Method 4: The compensation method

This one is perfect for simplifying mental maths and supporting students who feel anxious about borrowing. It uses friendly numbers to make the process feel more manageable.

Let's take 436 – 167 as an example:

First, round 167 up to 170 and subtract: 436 – 170 = 266
Then, add back the 3 you rounded up: 266 + 3 = 269

By adjusting the numbers slightly and then compensating, we avoid the stress of borrowing altogether. This is especially helpful for learners who prefer straightforward, logical steps and it's a great way to build confidence.

Building confidence in division

Division can often feel even more anxiety-inducing than subtraction, especially for students who find times tables challenging or who experience processing difficulties. But with the right approach, we can help make division feel more manageable.

Method 1: Chunking (repeated subtraction)

A concrete way in for students who need structure, this method treats division as repeated subtraction. It can be a helpful alternative for students who struggle with the abstract nature of the standard bus stop algorithm.

Let's take 240 ÷ 48 as an example:

First, subtract 192 (which is 4 × 48): 240 − 192 = 48
Then subtract the remaining 48 (1 × 48): 48 − 48 = 0
Total: 5 groups of 48

By breaking the division down into smaller, familiar steps, students can build on skills they already have. This approach makes the process more concrete and less overwhelming, especially for learners who benefit from seeing maths unfold step by step. It's a great way to build confidence while reinforcing understanding.

Method 2: Fraction simplification approach

If your student understands how to simplify fractions but finds long division daunting, this method can feel much more approachable. It allows them to work step by step, building confidence as they go. (This method entirely depends upon whether the numbers simplify.)

Start by writing the division as a fraction:
$$\frac{240}{48}$$
Then simplify in stages:
$$\frac{240}{48} \rightarrow \frac{120}{24}$$
$$\frac{120}{24} \rightarrow \frac{60}{12}$$
$$\frac{60}{12} \rightarrow \frac{30}{6}$$
$$\frac{30}{6} \rightarrow \frac{15}{3}$$
$$\frac{15}{3} \rightarrow \frac{5}{1}$$

The final answer simplifies to 5.

Allowing for these intermediate steps gives students time to process and check their thinking. It's a great way to reinforce number relationships and reduce the pressure that often comes with more formal division methods.

Method 3: Ratio/proportion table

This method is a great choice for students who are confident with doubling and prefer working within a table structure. It offers a structured, visual way into division that feels easier for those who find times tables challenging.

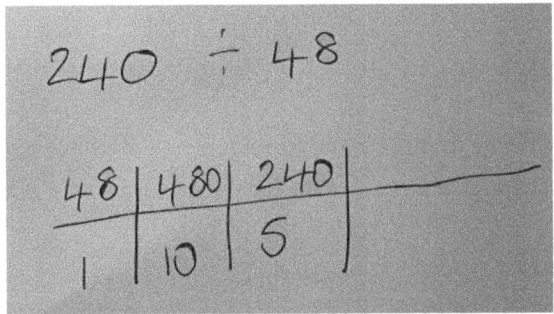

Figure 6.8 Ratio table showing systematic doubling approach to division.

Instead of relying on memorised facts, students build up to the answer by using what they already know. For example, they might start with 1 × 48 or 10 × 48, double to 2 × 48, 4 × 48, and so on – until they reach the target number. This step-by-step approach helps learners feel more in control and reduces the pressure that often comes with traditional division methods. The example shows the student multiplying by 10 and then halving to get 5 times the number.

By focusing on known facts rather than memorisation, students can approach division in a way that suits their strengths. It's a calm, logical method that builds confidence and reinforces number relationships along the way. I would add that ratio tables have an extensive use for learners who struggle with traditional approaches.

Script box: Introducing alternative methods

When a student says: 'I can't do multiplication. I've never been able to do it.'

- Say this: 'I get that! It can be tricky, but the great news is that there are lots of ways to multiply numbers. Let's explore one method that many of my students find more manageable than the usual one!'
- Not this: 'Everyone can learn multiplication if they try hard enough. Let's just review the standard method again.'
- Follow-up: 'Which of these methods feels the most comfortable for you? Let's practice that one together.'

Building your method repertoire

Having a range of methods is a brilliant starting point but it's how we introduce them that really makes the difference. It works best when new approaches are shared gradually, with care and clarity. That's why a week-by-week plan can be so helpful: it gives everyone space to explore, reflect and grow.

- Start with estimation. In Week 1, encourage students to estimate before diving into calculations. This builds their number sense and helps them feel more confident checking their work.
- In Week 2, introduce an alternative method alongside the traditional one. Let students see that maths isn't one-size-fits-all.
- By Week 3, invite them to choose the method that feels most comfortable.
- And in Week 4, mix things up. Encourage flexibility by practising different methods in lessons. Students begin to see themselves as adaptable mathematicians, capable of switching strategies with ease.

This gentle progression helps students ease into learning without feeling overwhelmed. It's not just about methods, it's about building confidence through choice and ownership.

Spotting what works for each learner

Every student brings something different to the table. Some count on their fingers, some struggle with place value and others shine when they spot patterns. The key is to notice these signs and match them with methods that play to their strengths.

- If a student relies on finger counting, try visual approaches like the Vedic method or array models, which build on what they already do naturally.
- For those making place value errors, the grid method or partial products can make the structure of numbers more visible.
- If carrying and borrowing causes anxiety, methods like compensation or working with negative numbers can simplify things.
- Students who love spotting patterns often thrive with the Vedic method or ratio tables, which highlight mathematical relationships.
- For students with working memory challenges, visual methods and grids help reduce cognitive load.

- If motor skills are a barrier, try approaches that minimise writing – mental methods or Vedic techniques can be a great fit. A set of sticks would work just as well.
- And for those facing language barriers, pictorial methods can help without relying on words.

Confidence builder: For teachers trying something new

Trying out alternative methods as a teacher can feel like stepping into the unknown – but it doesn't have to be daunting. Start small. Pick one method and practise it with simpler numbers like 12 × 13. Create a reference card for yourself, and let your students know you're learning too.

Saying, 'I'm exploring new approaches myself,' builds trust. It shows students that growth is for everyone – not just them.

A key takeaway from John Hattie's work is that teachers should see themselves as 'evaluators of their own impact' (Hattie, 2009). This means we should constantly be assessing whether our teaching is working. If it's not, the most effective teachers will change their approach rather than simply repeating the same one with the same outcome.

Supporting diverse learning needs

Adapting your teaching to meet different needs doesn't mean changing your goal – it means changing your path. Whether you're working with EAL students, or learners with dyslexia, ADHD or severe maths anxiety, the aim is always to give every student choices.

Learning difference	Effective methods	Key adaptations	Why they help
EAL students	Visual methods, grid method, Vedic method	Vocabulary cards; use their native language first if possible	Helps understanding beyond just language
Dyslexia	Vedic method, visual approaches	Minimise copying, use clear visual layouts	Makes it easier to avoid number formation challenges
ADHD	Compensation methods, chunking	Break down tasks, use timers, include movement breaks	Simplifies tasks by reducing complexity

Learning difference	Effective methods	Key adaptations	Why they help
Processing difficulties	Concrete manipulatives first, grid method	Progress from physical to pictorial to abstract	Builds understanding step by step
Dyscalculia	Vedic method, pattern-based approaches	Visual counting, avoid rote memorisation	Focuses on comprehension rather than just recall
Working memory issues	Grid method, visual representations	Use chunked information, add external supports	Reduces cognitive load for easier processing
Severe maths anxiety	Student-choice methods, visual approaches	Let students control their learning, remove assessment pressure	Helps rebuild confidence

Opening up our questions

Once we've matched methods to individual needs, the next step is to think about how we ask questions. Even the most thoughtful method can fall flat if the question itself feels closed or intimidating. By shifting the way we frame problems, we open the door to confidence. It's not just about what we teach, it's about how we invite students into the conversation.

Instead of asking, 'What is 18 × 5?', try asking, 'Can you show me three different ways to calculate 18 × 5?' These kinds of questions invite exploration and reduce the pressure of quick recall.

So how do we start shifting our questioning style? It doesn't have to be a huge change – just a small tweak in how we phrase things can open up space for thinking. Here are a few examples of how a closed question can become an invitation to explore:

- **Closed:** 'Calculate 15% of 80.' → **Open:** 'What percentages of 80 can you calculate?'
- **Closed:** 'Solve $3x + 5 = 20$.' → **Open:** 'Create an equation where $x = 5$.'
- **Closed:** 'Find the area of this rectangle.' → **Open:** 'What shapes could have an area of 24 cm²?'
- **Closed:** 'Divide 240 by 48.' → **Open:** 'If 240 ÷ 48 = 5, explain why this makes sense.'

These shifts turn maths into a conversation, not a test. Students begin to see maths not as a test to pass, but as a conversation they can join. Let's take a look at how that might sound in a real classroom.

Classroom dialogue: Exploring multiple methods

Teacher: 'Today we're going to look at different ways to multiply. Who remembers how to calculate 23 × 42?'
Student 1: 'I use the column method, but I always mess up the carrying.'
Teacher: 'That's one valid approach. Would you like to see a method that doesn't use carrying?'
Student 2: 'Is that allowed in the exam?'
Teacher: 'Absolutely! Any valid method gets you the marks. Let me show you the grid method.' *(Demonstrates grid method)*
Student 1: 'That makes so much more sense to me! I can actually see why it works.'
Teacher: 'Excellent! Different methods work for different people. The best one is just the one that makes most sense to you.'

Spoof assessment: Building analysis skills

Spoof assessments (see Chapter 11) can be a powerful way to support anxious or resistant learners. By removing the pressure to perform and shifting the focus to analysis, students can build confidence and develop their assessment literacy in a low-stakes environment.

Teaching tip: Worked examples

Worked examples are another great scaffold, especially when they show more than one way to solve a problem. Including two or three different methods in a single example reinforces the idea that there's no one 'right' way to do maths. If it's mathematically valid, it counts.

Managing mixed-method classrooms

When students use different methods, it's not about getting everyone to work the same way; it's about celebrating the variety of thinking they bring. Try pairing students who use different approaches and encourage them to talk through their reasoning. This kind of peer discussion helps build understanding and gives quieter or less confident learners a chance to shine.

You could also introduce 'method expert' roles, where students who feel secure with a particular method help others learn it. Teaching builds confidence and deepens understanding for everyone involved. If students bring methods from home or previous schools, welcome it. Ask them to explain how they work, acknowledge the thinking behind it, and help them link it to what's being taught in class. This builds trust and shows students that their experiences matter.

Knowledge organisers (see Chapter 5) can really help here. They give students a clear overview of key concepts and methods, and make it easier to compare and connect different approaches. They're a great tool for helping students feel more secure and confident in their learning.

> **Teaching tip: Communicating messages**
>
> Let everyone involved (other teachers, support staff and families) know that you're using a range of mathematical methods on purpose. These approaches aren't just about helping students pick up marks; they're chosen to suit individual learning needs, encourage flexible thinking and build confidence in maths. Sharing this message helps create a consistent and encouraging environment around the student. It reassures others that different methods are being used thoughtfully.

This kind of flexibility and clarity in the classroom also sets students up for success in assessments.

Assessment and GCSE connections

The flexible, inclusive approach used in the classroom doesn't just support learning, it also aligns with how GCSE maths is assessed. Across all major exam boards students are rewarded for showing clear reasoning, using valid methods and communicating their maths effectively; the Assessment Objectives. It's not about sticking to one set way; it's about making the thinking visible.

Students can use different methods to reach the correct answer, and as long as their approach is mathematically sound, they'll earn method marks. This is especially important for learners who may not use the most formal method but still demonstrate understanding. What matters is clarity, logic and accuracy.

This is reflected in examiner reports, available from all exam boards, which offer useful insights into how students approach questions and where they tend to go wrong:

- The column addition main error was not aligning the decimal point, with other common errors being arithmetic slips.

- The most common approach was to find the pay for one hour and then multiply by 15 but students who halved it and added were equally successful. Mistakes were usually arithmetic slips.

- Some students used a formal method whilst others used alternatives equally successfully.

- Students were required to show their workings as it is a 'show that' question, but many simply completed it.

- Numerical skills were poor. Students knew the required operation but were unable to carry it out accurately.

- Many students showed their work in a clear and logical way including checking results.

These examiner comments remind us how important it is for students to show their thinking clearly – whatever method they use. In GCSE maths, any valid mathematical approach can gain marks, as long as the reasoning is sound and the answer is correct. That flexibility is built into the mark schemes, but it's not always made explicit to students or teachers, which can lead to confusion or unnecessary pressure to stick to one method.

That's why it's so important to keep reinforcing the message: what matters most is understanding and clarity. Helping students feel confident in expressing their mathematical ideas, analysing errors and exploring different approaches builds not just competence, but trust in their own thinking. The more methods students encounter, the more they begin to see maths as something they can navigate, not just something they have to get through. That shift in mindset moves learners from feeling boxed in by one way of working to recognising that there are lots of valid paths to success.

Building mathematical flexibility

The journey from feeling resistant to becoming resilient often starts with a lightbulb moment: when a student realises that maths has so many different ways to succeed. Your role is to provide those pathways and help students find their unique mathematical voice. Your role is not to like or dislike any particular method – it might just be the method that the student can use efficiently.

Jo Morgan explores this beautifully in *A Compendium of Mathematical Methods*, where she notes that there are few, if any, longitudinal studies showing one method to be superior to another (Morgan, 2019). Her work offers valuable insight into how multiple methods can be implemented thoughtfully, and the considerations that come with that. By offering a range of approaches, we're not just teaching maths – we're showing students that it can be as rich and expressive as poetry, with countless ways to communicate the same idea.

> **Hear from the expert: Jo Morgan, Resourceaholic**
>
> 'Some of the very best maths teachers are those who take the time to research their subject in greater depth. Exploring new methods can help us make sense of things and deepen our mathematical understanding, even if we choose not to teach those methods. And sometimes it can be a revelation – I'll never forget the first time I discovered a new way to find the highest common factor. I was so excited by it, and to this day my students benefit from the fact that I opened my eyes to new methods.'

Adapting to your setting

- **GCSE classrooms:** Link multiplication methods to algebraic expressions – for example, show how the grid method connects to expanding brackets like $(x + 3)(x + 2)$. Make method choice part of everyday practice so students see the connections across topics.
- **Resit students:** Frame new methods as fresh starts, not as remedial fixes. Remind students that past difficulties often reflect a mismatch in methods – not a lack of ability. You could create method portfolios where students record which approaches work best for different types of problems.
- **Vocational support contexts:** Use examples that link directly to learners' trades—like measurements in construction or quantities in catering. When methods feel relevant to the job, learners are more likely to engage and remember them.
- **One-to-one intervention:** Start with hands-on activities using manipulatives before moving to pictures and numbers, give students pre-prepared grids or frames to fill in. Give students time to explore different methods at their own pace – there's no rush. The goal is for them to feel confident choosing what works best for them.
- **Adult learners:** Be mindful of the anxiety some adults carry from previous maths experiences. When introducing new methods, connect them to real-life contexts – like using the grid method to calculate material costs for a DIY project. Relevance builds confidence.
- **Functional Skills contexts:** Alternative methods fit naturally with the practical focus of Functional Skills. Chunking for division mirrors how problems are tackled in the workplace – breaking tasks into manageable steps. Grid multiplication is great for calculating material quantities, showing that these are real-world techniques, not just simplified ones.
- **Students with severe maths anxiety:** Begin with visual methods that feel less intimidating. Let students choose how they want to tackle problems, and

consider creating 'anxiety-free zones' where they can explore maths without the pressure of assessments. A calm, flexible approach can make a big difference.

Key research points

- John Hattie: *Visible Learning*
  - Key idea: If a student doesn't grasp a concept through one method, it's more effective to try a different approach than to repeat the same explanation.
  - Use it: When a student is stuck, switch it up. Offer a different method straight away rather than going over the same one again.
- Steve Chinn: *Mathematics for Dyscalculia and SEND Learners*
  - Key idea: If a student can't figure something out the first way, keep offering alternatives until one clicks.
  - Use it: Have a few go-to methods ready for each operation so you can help students explore different ways of working.
- *Cognitive Load Theory* (The Education Hub, 2019)
  - Key idea: Our working memory can only handle a few new pieces of information at once – typically 3 to 4.
  - Use it: Offering alternative methods can reduce overload by connecting new learning to what students already know and feel confident with.

Reflection questions

- Which students might thrive with some alternative methods?
- How will you introduce method choices without making it overwhelming?
- What strategies do you have in place to support students who are hesitant to try something new?
- How can offering these various methods boost student confidence and resilience in your teaching environment?

Next steps

- This week: Pick one alternative method to try with your most reluctant students and see how they respond – check in on their confidence levels too!
- This month: Design or co-create with students a classroom display featuring different solutions to the same problem, celebrating the wonderful diversity in maths!
- This term: Gather examples of student work that showcase different methods. Share these success stories and build a portfolio of effective strategies.
- This year: Collaborate with your department to agree on 2–3 alternative methods that everyone will offer, making sure you keep things consistent but flexible. Reference Jo Morgan's *Compendium of Mathematical Methods*.

Part Three

Creating Connections

Chapter 7
Vocational and Real-life Relevance

From 'When will I ever use this?' to 'I can see why this matters'

'When am I ever going to need algebra, Miss?' It's a question we've all heard. And it's a fair one. Do you have a convincing response ready – one that shows how maths connects to everyday life and professional success across industries?

According to National Numeracy over half of employers (53 per cent) know that some employees have weaker numeracy skills (National Numeracy, 2019). This is especially true in jobs like retail, hospitality and transportation, where 68 per cent of companies say numeracy gaps are common.

We've already seen that relevance is one of the biggest barriers to learning. Robey and Jones found that students are far more engaged and positive when they can see how maths and English relate to their own lives (Robey and Jones, 2015). It's about making personal connections and giving feedback that links learning directly to their qualifications and goals.

Let's take that insight further by exploring strategies like Realistic Maths Education (RME), cross-curricular approaches, and project-based learning (PBL). Research shows that these methods can make a real difference.

How can we connect maths to real-life situations in a way that feels genuine?

Whether it's during T Level placements, internships or part-time jobs, even a small mathematical mistake can have serious consequences – financial losses for employers, missed opportunities for students and, in some cases, safety risks.

There are plenty of real-world examples to share with students. A misplaced decimal point once made a submarine 'too overweight to float', costing €2 billion to fix (Tech Startups, 2020). The Mars Rover mission failed due to a unit conversion error: one team used inches, the other centimetres, and no one double-checked (LA Times, 1999). These stories help students see why accuracy in maths really matters.

It might seem like just numbers and formulas, but in the real world, mistakes can have serious consequences.

- In construction, a small decimal error in concrete calculations can compromise the strength of a building. If angles aren't measured correctly during bridge construction, the pieces won't fit and the whole project could be delayed or scrapped. Misjudging material quantities can waste thousands of pounds and push deadlines back.
- In healthcare, incorrect medication dosages can put lives at risk. A miscalculated IV drip rate or a misread statistic could lead to the wrong treatment being given. Accuracy isn't optional – it's essential.
- In business, a pricing error could bankrupt a small company. Investment miscalculations can affect pensions and financial security. Even basic supply chain maths can be the difference between profit and loss.
- In engineering, the collapse of the Tacoma Narrows Bridge is a well-known example of poor mathematical modelling. Software errors – often maths-related – have led to car recalls. And if load calculations for buildings are wrong, the results can be catastrophic.

Sharing these stories with students helps them understand that mathematical accuracy isn't just about passing exams – it's about protecting lives, saving money and making smart decisions.

Teaching tip: Making consequences real

Help students connect mathematical accuracy to their own vocational context. A simple four-week structure can make this feel purposeful and personal:

- Week 1: Research real mathematical errors in their chosen vocational field.
- Week 2: Calculate how these mistakes could impact finances or safety in the workplace.
- Week 3: Meet with local employers to discuss expectations around maths skills. Even better – invite them into the classroom or create a vlog.
- Week 4: Present findings, linking mathematical accuracy to career prospects.

> This approach helps students see consequences not as distant or dramatic, but as directly relevant to their future. It builds motivation by showing that maths isn't just about getting the right answer – it's about being trusted, capable and employable.

Seamlessly embedding mathematics in vocational training

Schools and colleges are focused on preparing skilled professionals – whether that's a brilliant chef, a creative hairdresser or a compassionate care worker. But vocational instructors often face a challenge: how to integrate maths and English into their courses without it feeling forced or disconnected. This tension is real, especially for educators juggling dual roles.

The National Research and Development Council (NRDC) for adult literacy and numeracy report *'You wouldn't expect a maths teacher to teach plastering'* (Casey et al., 2006) explored how embedding English and maths into vocational training works across different fields. It highlighted both the benefits and the challenges. So, what does embedding actually mean? It's about using every opportunity to help students develop their maths skills through their vocational subjects – whether that's art and design, PE or construction.

The NRDC findings were encouraging. Embedded courses showed:

- higher student retention
- more positive attitudes toward literacy and numeracy
- greater success in vocational qualifications – especially at level 2
- maths and numeracy achievement rates of 93 per cent, compared to 73 per cent in non-embedded courses
- students feeling better prepared for the workplace.

But there's a caveat: when one teacher was responsible for both vocational and maths/English delivery, students were twice as likely to struggle. This shows that structure alone isn't enough – we also need the right attitudes and support systems to make embedding work.

Vocational staff don't need advanced qualifications in maths or English to support their students – but a solid grasp of the basics helps them make meaningful connections. Sometimes, staff may not realise they have gaps in their own skills, which can make them hesitant to engage with maths and English training. Others may have undiagnosed learning needs and have developed coping strategies that work in the workplace but feel uncomfortable bringing those challenges into the classroom.

It's important to remember: if vocational staff aren't confident with certain concepts, they won't be able to embed them into their teaching. Giving them access to the curriculum and dedicated time with maths and English specialists can make a big difference. This kind of collaboration helps students experience those valuable cross-subject connections more naturally.

Some staff may not fully recognise the importance of embedding these skills and many find maths harder to integrate than English. That's why consistent messaging across the organisation is key, along with training that meets everyone's needs. Like many maths teachers, vocational staff often teach maths the way they learned it themselves.

That said, many are open to exploring new approaches. Ratio tables, for example, have proven particularly effective for vocational staff, as highlighted in the Centre for Excellence in Mathematics Education and Training Foundation (CfEM) study (Zarnadze, 2023). When staff see how these tools work in their own context, they're more likely to use them confidently.

Practical collaboration strategies

Building strong partnerships between vocational and maths staff doesn't need to be complicated. A simple four-week structure can help you start small and grow confidence over time.

Collaboration stage	Time investment	Teacher actions	Expected outcomes	Troubleshooting
Week 1: Discovery	15 minutes	Ask: 'What calculations do your students struggle with?'	Identify 2–3 specific mathematical challenges.	If your colleague seems resistant, start by focusing on their expertise.
Week 2: Observation	1 lesson	Watch where mathematical thinking appears naturally.	Map existing mathematical moments.	If no maths is visible, ask about problem-solving approaches.
Week 3: Joint planning	30 minutes	Plan a shared activity – vocational lead, maths support.	One collaboratively designed lesson.	Start small: enhance an existing activity rather than create something new.
Week 4: Evaluation	15 minutes	Review what worked and adapt for the next cycle.	A sustainable collaboration model.	Celebrate small wins – don't expect transformation overnight.

Even modest collaboration can lead to meaningful change. When vocational and maths staff work together, students benefit from more joined-up learning and staff feel more confident embedding maths in ways that feel natural and relevant.

Maths careers exploration

Help students see the real-world value of maths by linking it directly to their career interests. Use visual prompts and personalised research to make the connections feel tangible and motivating.

Use maths careers posters (see Further Reading and Resources) like:

- 'What's the point of Pythagoras?'
- 'What's the point of prime numbers?'
- 'When will I ever need this… maths in art?'

These posters link maths to subjects like art, geography and PE, and show how it's used in architecture, music and navigation. They're great conversation starters and help students see maths in places they hadn't considered.

Embedding or enhancing? A philosophical shift

Let's talk about a subtle but important distinction: embedding versus enhancing. Embedding often feels like we're trying to hide maths inside vocational content, sometimes awkwardly. Enhancement, on the other hand, is about building on what's already there. It's about recognising the maths that's naturally present in vocational subjects and helping it shine.

In a podcast with the English and Maths Booth, I made the case for enhancement. Every course contains maths – it's already there (English and Maths Booth, 2021). Our job is to help students grow their skills by making those connections visible and meaningful. The outcomes speak for themselves. When embedding is done just for the sake of it, it can feel artificial. I remember visiting a hairdressing academy where students were measuring doors and pavements to design a disabled ramp. It felt like the activity had been created just for my visit – and it didn't seem relevant to their training. These kinds of experiences can confuse students more than they help. Enhancement means working with what's real and relevant. That's more than enough.

> **Student voice: Spotting fake relevance**
>
> Sometimes, students see straight through the scenarios we create – and when that happens, it can undermine trust and engagement.
>
> - 'Miss, could we work on some real-life percentages? I actually work in retail, and I think our calculations are a bit different from the shop problems we're using.' – Year 11 business student
> - 'I really wish teachers would ask us about the maths we actually use at our weekend jobs instead of these made-up scenarios.' – catering student
>
> When students feel the maths they're being taught doesn't reflect their real experiences, it's harder for them to believe in its value. That's why authenticity matters.

Making maths meaningful in vocational contexts

Vocational learners often use maths every day whether they realise it or not. The key is to help them recognise and build on that existing competence. When maths is clearly connected to their chosen field, it feels relevant, empowering and worth learning.

Here are some examples of how maths shows up naturally across vocational areas:

- **Hairdressing and beauty:** Mixing hair colour requires precise ratios, and timing treatments demands accurate time calculations – often using both digital and analogue clocks. Geometry is used in cutting angles and analysing facial symmetry, while cash handling and commission calculations build financial fluency.
- **Construction:** Pythagoras is commonly known as the '3, 4, 5 rule' for creating perfect right angles. Students often convert directly from millimetres to metres, skipping centimetres entirely – leading to common error patterns. Material quantities, cost estimation and angle calculations are all part of everyday tasks.
- **Catering:** Maths is used to scale recipes, control portions, calculate food costs and monitor temperatures. These skills are essential for profitability and food safety.
- **Health and social care:** Medication dosages, interpreting health statistics, managing shift schedules and calculating BMI all require mathematical thinking. Accuracy here can directly impact patient safety.

These examples aren't just 'real-world', they're the world your students are preparing to enter. By designing activities that reflect these authentic applications, you help students see maths as a tool they already use and can continue to master.

Confidence builder: Understanding cross-curricular mathematics

To support this work, it helps to refresh your understanding of how maths connects across subjects. These cross-curricular links can strengthen your confidence and make your teaching more responsive:

- **Measurement** (or mensuration in geometry) appears in almost every practical subject – through length, area, weight, volume and time.
- **Percentages** feature in business calculations, health statistics and efficiency measures.
- **Ratio and proportion** underpin recipe work, mixing solutions, scaling designs and conversions.
- **Statistics** help interpret data in science, geography and business studies.

The more confident you are in spotting these connections, the more naturally they'll transfer to your students.

The MEI has created a fantastic contextualisation toolkit that shows how maths can blend seamlessly with vocational programmes (see Further Reading and Resources). It helps you find meaningful connections across courses and make learning more engaging.

Building authentic workplace connections

Following on from identifying maths in vocational and cross-curricular contexts, the next step is helping students see how these skills show up in their everyday lives – especially in work and home settings. When students recognise that they're already using maths outside the classroom, it builds confidence and shifts the narrative from 'I can't do maths' to 'I already do maths.'

> **Classroom activity: Real mathematical lives discovery**
>
> 1 Give students sticky notes and ask: 'Write down three ways you used numbers, calculations or mathematical thinking in the last 48 hours – not school maths, real-life maths.'
> 2 Students post their notes on the board and group similar responses. You'll typically see:
>   - money calculations (budgeting, shopping, wages)
>   - time management (shifts, travel, appointments)
>   - measurement (cooking, DIY, exercise)
>   - data interpretation (social media stats, health monitoring).
> 3 Celebrate the mathematical sophistication revealed: 'This is advanced mathematical thinking – you're already mathematicians.'
>
> Why this works: it helps students see themselves as capable and competent. They realise they're already doing complex maths in familiar contexts, which builds confidence and motivation.

Script box: Connecting to family or domestic mathematical experience

When a student says: 'My dad didn't need maths – he left school at 15 and now runs his own building company!'

- Say this: 'That's brilliant – have you ever asked him about the maths he uses in his work? Try asking him about the 3, 4, 5 rule in bricklaying – that's actually Pythagoras' theorem!'
- Not this: 'Well, you can't leave school until you're 18 and you have to keep doing maths until you get Grade 4.'
- Follow-up: Encourage students to chat with their parents, carers or employers about the maths they use day-to-day. You could also reach out to families – send a message home inviting them to share how maths shows up in their work or everyday life.

This is a great chance for students to celebrate the amazing maths thinking happening in their families, no matter the job or background. It's a powerful way to show how maths is woven into all kinds of real-life experiences.

Paul Wassan is the Catering and Hospitality Manager at Market Field College (a specialist college for students with learning difficulties). He has developed a brilliantly intuitive approach to supporting students with their maths skills without ever using the word 'maths'. By embedding mathematical thinking into real-life culinary experiences, he makes learning practical, sensory and engaging. His method allows students to build confidence through hands-on vocational tasks that feel relevant and rewarding.

In his kitchen classroom, maths is experienced through the senses. Students count gas clicks to light a stove (hearing), adjust temperatures based on smell, compare heat levels by touch, divide traybakes by sight and assess food quality through taste. These everyday tasks naturally introduce concepts like measurement, timing, division and problem solving – without the need for formal maths language.

His students apply maths in meaningful ways: calculating washing temperatures for uniforms, planning cooking schedules, scaling recipes from one sandwich to 70 and analysing feedback like the crispiness of bacon to adjust heat levels. These activities build mathematical understanding through relevance and repetition.

Hear from the expert: Paul Wassan, Catering and Hospitality Manager, Market Field College

'When you embed maths into a vocational subject, you're already halfway there. Students have chosen the subject – they want to be there – which removes a big barrier. It's practical, hands-on and active. Plus, there's an end product they can see, touch, taste and feel. That makes the learning real.

As SEN providers – and really, as all teachers – getting to know our students is key. Every learner has their own quirks and habits, so connection is essential. At the start of the year, I always sit down with them for a cup of tea and maybe a biscuit. That chat grows over the three years they're with us, and it lays the foundation for everything that follows.'

Paul's approach shows how authentic, meaningful maths can emerge naturally when we build on what students are already doing – rather than forcing abstract content into vocational contexts.

Teaching tip: Vocational embedding wheel for vocational teachers

Use this wheel in a 30-minute collaborative session with vocational colleagues to help uncover authentic maths connections – not just bolt-ons.

1 **Choose a typical unit** from the course and break it down into its modules.
2 **On flip chart paper**, draw a central circle and divide it into sections – one for each module. In each section, jot down what's being taught (e.g. Health and safety signs, PPE, accident reporting).
3 **Add an outer wheel**, extending each module section outward.
4 **In this outer ring**, identify the maths or English that naturally shows up in each module. Be specific – instead of just saying 'averages', note *what kind* of averages and *where* they appear.
5 **Add another ring** to show what extra maths or English could be easily embedded into each module.
6 This gives you a clear picture of where specialist input (maths/English) can be most effectively targeted.
7 **Outside the wheel**, note any maths or English topics that don't appear at all in the module – this helps clarify what *doesn't* need embedding.

This tool is a great way to make maths and English feel relevant and purposeful – rooted in the real work students are preparing for.

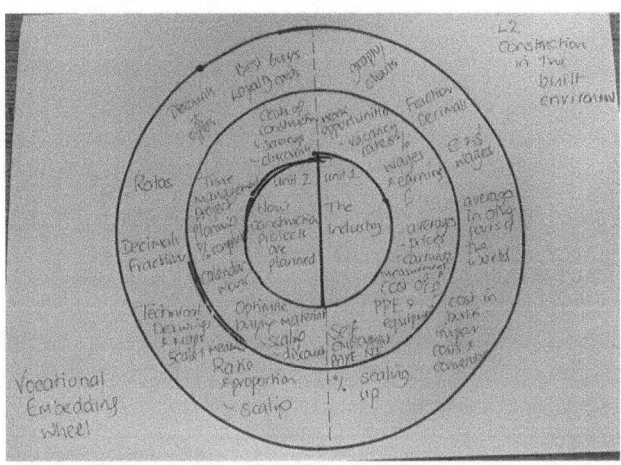

Figure 7.1 The Vocational Embedding Wheel.

T Levels and work-based learning integration

At the time of writing, T Levels offer a powerful blend of classroom learning and real-world experience, with students spending at least nine weeks on placement. When it comes to vocational embedding, all the same principles apply – and it's especially important that T Levels reflect current industry practice.

Strong employer engagement is key. It helps students succeed and supports what the NRDC calls 'crucial attitudinal features' – the beliefs and values that shape how learners see maths and its relevance.

One thing to watch out for: if an employer has a negative view of maths, their intern or placement student might pick up on that too. That's why it's so important to highlight the value of good maths skills alongside technical expertise during employer engagement events.

Making maths part of the T Level journey

Before placement

- Students can research the maths skills relevant to their roles.
- They can practise using real workplace data to build confidence.
- Create a low-pressure space where they can strengthen their maths skills.

During placement (weekly check-ins)

- Students track the maths they notice and use in their day-to-day tasks.
- They identify any gaps between classroom learning and workplace needs.
- You gather evidence of how their maths skills are developing in context.

After placement (back at college)

- Students share what they've learned about workplace maths with peers.
- Assessment can focus on how authentically they apply their maths knowledge.
- The curriculum can be adapted to reflect the real-life maths they encountered.

By making maths feel approachable and relevant, you're helping students build confidence not just in their technical skills, but in their ability to think mathematically in the real world.

Cross-curricular and whole-school approaches

In a thriving school or college culture, maths and English aren't just the responsibility of specialist teams – they're part of everyone's toolkit. The same goes for supporting additional learning needs (ALN): it's a shared commitment, not just the SENCo's domain.

Of course, some staff may feel unsure about their own maths skills – and that's completely understandable. With the right support, we can help colleagues build confidence in the basics, which in turn strengthens their ability to support learners.

One way to do this is by connecting maths to subjects staff already feel passionate about – like PE, geography, DT or catering – where maths is already embedded in the content. Coaching models show us that *success builds success*, and these natural connections can lead to quick wins and a ripple effect across departments.

To build on this momentum, consider establishing Maths Staff Champions: colleagues who lead on promoting maths across the curriculum. Include learning support staff too; many are keen to develop professionally, and growing talent from within is especially valuable in times of recruitment challenges. High-impact CPD focused on practical mathematical methods (rather than heavy content) can make a real difference – not just for staff confidence, but for whole-school/college culture.

Once staff begin to feel more confident and supported, you can start to build a wider mathematical culture across the school or college. Here's a simple, sustainable way to get started:

- **Month 1:** Identify enthusiastic staff in maths-rich subjects (PE, geography, DT, construction, catering).

- **Month 2:** Offer a 1-hour CPD session introducing accessible mathematical methods.

- **Month 3:** Support joint lessons that showcase natural mathematical connections.

- **Month 4:** Celebrate successes and invite more departments to get involved.

Focus on *enhancing* what's already happening, rather than adding extra workload. Help staff recognise and build on the mathematical thinking they're already supporting – often without even realising it.

Evidence-based pedagogical approaches

When it comes to engaging students who may feel disconnected from maths, especially those resitting GCSEs or learning in vocational contexts, it's worth exploring approaches that are grounded in research and proven to work. Two powerful methods stand out: Realistic Maths Education (RME) and project-based learning (PBL).

Realistic Maths Education (RME)

RME originated in the Netherlands and focuses on making maths meaningful by always rooting it in real-life situations. It's gained traction internationally, including in the USA and the UK, where a major study by Dickinson and Hough explored its impact across Key Stages 3 and 4, and post-16 learners (Dickinson and Hough, 2012). The approach has since inspired a rich collection of resources (see Further Reading and Resources).

RME is particularly effective for students who feel reluctant or resistant about maths – especially those retaking GCSEs. It tackles common barriers like disengagement, confusion and low confidence by:

- **Making maths relevant:** Students explore scenarios they recognise, like planning shopping trips, managing stock or budgeting, helping them see the value of maths in everyday life.

- **Encouraging problem solving**: Instead of memorising rules, students think critically and reason through problems, which builds confidence and independence.

- **Focusing on deep understanding**: RME prioritises conceptual clarity over surface-level learning, helping students build a solid foundation they can apply elsewhere.

- **Using visual tools**: Diagrams and drawings help students make sense of abstract ideas, offering flexible ways to approach problems.

- **Boosting confidence**: Research shows that students using RME not only improve their maths skills but also feel more capable and positive about learning.

- **Creating active classrooms**: Students discuss familiar situations, work collaboratively, and share strategies – making learning more interactive and less isolating.

- **Valuing the process:** In RME, the journey matters as much as the answer. For example, in a stock control task, students explore how a real-world situation becomes a maths problem – reducing fear of mistakes and encouraging curiosity.

In short, RME helps break down barriers by making maths feel relevant, collaborative and empowering. It's especially useful in vocational settings, where simple swaps can make a big difference:

- replace abstract train timetable problems with shift scheduling tasks
- swap generic shopping scenarios for inventory management exercises
- turn holiday budgeting into practical planning for course materials or equipment.

Project-based learning (PBL)

PBL is another powerful approach that brings learning to life. Originating in the USA, it centres on real-world problems and encourages students to think critically, solve challenges and work collaboratively. It's especially effective in vocational and creative settings, where hands-on experience matters.

In 2012, I had the opportunity to visit High Tech High in San Diego (a world-class PBL school), thanks to The Goldsmiths Foundation. Students were immersed in authentic projects: building boats, designing marketing materials, running a hydroponic farm and more. The energy and engagement were incredible.

PBL integrates a wide range of subjects – maths, English, creativity, leadership – and while some core maths standards may need to be supported through traditional methods, the flexibility of PBL allows students to thrive.

For learners who've struggled with maths, completing a meaningful project can be transformative:

- **real outcomes** drive motivation more than exams
- **teamwork** builds confidence and reduces anxiety
- **community involvement** connects students to real-world impact.

Projects that work well often address genuine community needs. For example:

- creating mathematical tools for local businesses
- developing budget planning resources for community groups
- conducting efficiency analyses for organisations
- designing maths training materials for younger students.

PBL also benefits from dynamic learning environments – workshops, presentation spaces, and creative zones – which suit students who don't thrive in traditional classrooms. It's a space for inspirational, creative thinking, and for many it's where they finally feel seen and successful.

Functional Skills integration

For students who've struggled with GCSE maths, Functional Skills offer a fresh and practical way back into learning. They can be used as a stepping stone into GCSE resits depending upon the student's original grade in Year 11. Instead of focusing solely on abstract theory, Functional Skills show students how maths works in real-life situations – answering that familiar question: 'When will I ever use this?' Vocationally relevant scenarios apply equally well to both GCSE and Functional Skills maths pathways. Here's why:

- Direct relevance to life and work: Functional Skills are designed to be career-ready. They bridge the gap between classroom learning and the demands of everyday life and employment. Students begin to see how maths applies to budgeting, planning, measuring and problem solving – all things they'll encounter in work and life.
- Tiered progression: the qualification structure (from Entry Level 1 through to Level 2) offers clear, achievable milestones:
  - Entry Level 1 focuses on basic calculations and simple problem solving, ideal for students aiming for part-time jobs or entry-level roles.
  - Level 2 introduces more complex tasks, preparing students for supervisory positions or further study.

  This step-by-step approach allows learners to build confidence gradually, celebrating success at each stage rather than facing a single high-stakes exam.
- Flexible and student-centred assessment: Functional Maths exams are designed to be taken when the student is ready, with multiple windows available throughout the academic year. This flexibility helps reduce pressure and supports genuine readiness – not just exam survival.
- Employer-driven relevance: Functional Skills were developed in response to calls from the Confederation of British Industry (CBI), who wanted students to leave education with stronger, more applicable maths skills. These are the skills employers are asking for and they're built into the heart of the qualification.

Bringing Functional Skills to life

To make maths feel truly relevant, consider embedding tasks that reflect real-world scenarios students might encounter in their lives or future careers:

- Budgeting for a household or small business: Covers calculations, percentages and average wages.
- Calculating materials for a DIY or craft project: Involves measurement, area and practical problem solving.
- Analysing sales figures or tracking personal finances: Applies data interpretation, ratios and graphical representation.

By explicitly linking maths concepts to these kinds of tasks you help students see the immediate value of what they're learning. It's not just about passing an exam; it's about preparing for life. These two classroom activities are designed to bridge that gap – using real data and everyday situations to make maths feel relevant, purposeful and engaging.

Classroom activity: Real workplace data investigation

Instead of artificial scenarios, give students real problems to explore using genuine data. This activity connects directly to their career goals and helps them answer questions they genuinely care about.

What students can investigate:

- typical starting salaries in their chosen field
- the financial impact of different qualification levels
- regional variations in employment opportunities
- news stories linked to their vocational interests.

Implementation steps:

- Week 1: Students choose a topic relevant to their future career.
- Week 2: Research using authentic sources (e.g. Office for National Statistics (ONS), job sites, company reports).
- Week 3: Analyse and interpret the data mathematically.
- Week 4: Present findings to an authentic audience (younger students, vocational staff, employers).

This activity uses real data to answer real questions, not just questions created for maths practice. It builds confidence, relevance and a sense of ownership over learning.

Once students have explored data linked to their career goals, you can extend the conversation by showing how maths appears in everyday life, often in places they don't expect. This helps reinforce the idea that maths isn't just for school or work; it's everywhere.

Classroom activity: Everyday maths in the news

Use newspapers, magazines or online articles to help students spot maths in the world around them. This shared reading activity encourages curiosity and builds confidence in interpreting real-world information. Look for percentages, fractions, kilometres, graphs, averages, currency amounts (£, $, €), sales offers, house prices, inflation and earnings.

Connect findings to vocational areas (e.g. construction students: house prices, building industry news, material costs; health students: healthcare statistics, demographic trends, NHS funding; business students: economic indicators, retail performance, start-up success rates).

Stick to everyday situations: imagining new scenarios can be tricky, especially for SEND learners. Use real objects, packaging or pictures with minimal text to support understanding and make the activity inclusive.

AQA's proposed numeracy qualification – designed to reflect real-world maths like overdrafts, budgeting and employment – has also sparked interest. Be realistic: most 14–19 year-olds aren't dealing with mortgages or pensions. The content feels aspirational, not accessible. What it does highlight, though, is that the system is trying to respond. And that reinforces what we've said all along: if we focus on fluency, fundamental facts, confidence with tools, and tackling maths anxiety, outcomes improve. The 5Rs approach still stands. Whatever new qualifications emerge, these foundations remain essential.

Supporting implementation

Even with the best intentions and planning, embedding maths authentically can come with its challenges. That's completely normal and it's where a bit of curiosity, collaboration and gentle persistence can go a long way.

Here are some common bumps in the road, and how you might navigate them:

- **'We can't find authentic examples.'** Start with what students already know. Their part-time jobs, hobbies or family businesses often contain rich mathematical thinking. Bring those experiences into the classroom and connect them to formal concepts. When students say, *'This is like what I actually do,'* you know you're on the right track.

- **'Vocational staff aren't engaging.'** Begin by noticing and celebrating what's already working. Observe without judgement, highlight good practice and offer support that feels manageable. Sometimes, a small win like helping a colleague address a basic maths skill they've been quietly avoiding can open the door to deeper collaboration.

- **'Students say "this isn't real maths."'** Make the maths visible. Connect it to the curriculum, show how it links to progression routes and validate the complexity of what they're doing. When students start using mathematical language confidently, you'll see their mindset shift.

- **'I don't understand the vocational context.'** That's okay, you don't have to be the expert. Be a learner alongside your students. Ask genuine questions, listen carefully and partner with vocational colleagues. Use industry resources to deepen your understanding. Authentic questions lead to authentic discussions and that's where the magic happens.

Adapting to your setting

- **GCSE classrooms:** Some students will not have entered the world of work, and some will be unable to do so; for them, this type of link is aspirational. Focus more upon real-life maths such as budgeting, deals and discounts, saving money with best buys and using the student discount card.
- **Resit students:** Again, the world of work may be aspirational, but some students will face the opposite issue, where they are going to college and then going straight to their part-time job. Some will face copious financial pressures. Use real-life data such as minimum wage, tips, saving and the lived experience of your students.
- **Vocational support contexts:** Use examples that link directly to work, employment and prospects and reinforce the value of good maths qualifications.
- **One-to-one intervention:** Start with lived experience, aspirations and dreams. Use everyday scenarios and encourage discussion and exploration of maths in the news, on favourite television programmes and in daily life.

- **Adult learners:** Be mindful of financial pressures and aspirational work. Remind students of the benefits of further study and maths qualifications which will hopefully open doors.
- **Functional Skills contexts:** Use real-life scenarios and real-life artefacts such as measuring jugs, packaging, adverts.
- **Students with severe maths anxiety:** Recognise the anxiety and support students in co-creating maths scenarios that they could explore.

Key research points

- Robey and Jones: *Engaging Learners in GCSE Maths and English*
  - Key takeaway: Personal relevance must be made explicit and clearly linked to qualification goals.
  - Use it: Make sure every maths concept is connected to something that matters to your students – their goals, their interests, their future.
- NRDC (2006): *'You wouldn't expect a maths teacher to teach plastering'*
  - Key takeaway: Collaboration between maths and vocational specialists is more effective than expecting one person to do both.
  - Use it: Work in partnership with vocational colleagues: you don't need to be the expert in their field, but you can bring the maths expertise to the table.
- Dickinson and Hough: *Using Realistic Mathematics Education in UK Classrooms* (Manchester Metropolitan University)
  - Key takeaway: Students taught through realistic contexts show improved accuracy and confidence compared to traditional approaches.
  - Use it: Swap out artificial word problems for real-life scenarios your students actually encounter – in work, in life and in their vocational areas.

Reflection questions

- What's already happening across your organisation to support maths?
- Is there a whole-setting approach like Numeracy across the curriculum? Where are the pockets of good practice and how could they be shared or scaled?
- Are you part of the conversation with vocational teams? Do you have regular input into vocational team meetings or staff training? If not, what would help make that happen?
- How well do you know what students are learning elsewhere? Are you familiar with the content of other courses? What could you do to build that understanding – and how might it help you embed maths more meaningfully?
- Where does maths already live in vocational areas? What kinds of mathematical thinking naturally appear in the subjects your students study? How can you make those connections more visible?

- Who could help bring maths to life for your students? Which local employers, community groups or organisations could offer authentic mathematical challenges? How might you start that conversation?

Next steps

1. **Start with what's real:** Use students' part-time jobs, hobbies or home experiences as the starting point for maths discussions. Authenticity builds trust and engagement.
2. **Collaborate with vocational staff:** Set up short, structured partnerships – even 30-minute planning sessions – to identify where maths already appears in vocational content and how it can be enhanced.
3. **Use employer voices to validate maths:** Invite local employers to discuss the maths they expect in the workplace. This helps students see the relevance and builds motivation through real-world expectations.
4. **Shift from embedding to enhancing:** Focus on recognising and amplifying the maths that's already present in vocational subjects. Enhancement feels more natural, more respectful – and more effective.

Chapter 8
Mathematical Hooks

From 'I can't see the point' to 'That's actually quite interesting'

'Miss, can you show us that picture again? The one with the spiral shells? I want to take a photo of it.'

This was a Year 10 student who, until that moment, had shown little interest in maths. But something had shifted. A simple image – spiral shells arranged in nature – had sparked a genuine sense of curiosity. What began as a standard lesson on proportion had turned into a moment of wonder, all thanks to a glimpse of the golden ratio and logarithmic spirals in the natural world.

These are the moments mathematical hooks can create. Whether it's a striking image, a short video, a hands-on demonstration or a real-world scenario, a good hook draws students in. It opens a door. Suddenly, maths isn't just about numbers and rules, it's about patterns, relationships and the surprising ways they show up in the world around us.

This chapter explores how to use mathematical hooks with purpose. It's about helping students move from disengagement to discovery, and showing that maths can be as creative, visual and meaningful as any other subject.

What makes a hook work?

So what makes a mathematical hook truly effective? It's not just about showing something interesting – it's about sparking a moment of recognition, a question, a connection. The best hooks are visually striking, rich in mathematical potential and accessible to all learners. They invite curiosity and open up space for discussion, exploration, and discovery.

Pete Mattock puts it well when he talks of models, such as bar models or dienes blocks: 'The only way to make sense of abstract concepts is to have models for them – models that can be seen, manipulated and reasoned with. No single model works for all occasions, but a good range of representations can unlock any maths concept.'

This translates well into using hooks too. In practice, this means choosing hooks that feel authentic and relevant. Students quickly sense when a mathematical link is forced. But when the connection is real – when the maths is embedded in something beautiful, familiar or surprising – they lean in.

Let's look at some of the richest sources of hooks:

- **Nature** offers endless examples: sunflower spirals, pine cones, nautilus shells, snowflakes and coastlines. These patterns reveal Fibonacci sequences, the golden ratio, fractals and geometric symmetry – all embedded in the world around us.

- **Art and architecture** bring maths into human creativity. From Islamic tessellations to Renaissance perspective, from modern buildings to optical illusions, students see how mathematical principles shape design, structure and visual impact.

- **Technology and innovation** connect maths to students' digital lives. Pixel resolution, gaming algorithms, social media analytics and even cryptocurrency all rely on mathematical thinking. These hooks show that maths powers the tools and platforms they use every day.

- **Sport and competition** appeal to active learners. Whether it's analysing Olympic records, calculating game probabilities or exploring the physics of movement, sport-based hooks make maths active and strategic.

Each of these areas offers more than just a 'wow' moment – they provide a doorway into meaningful mathematical thinking. And when students begin to see maths not as a separate subject, but as something woven into the things they already care about, the shift from 'I don't get it' to 'That's actually quite interesting' begins. It can help to make the most challenging of concepts much easier to comprehend.

Hear from the expert: Dr Ed Southall, Maths Lead, Oak Academy

'The pursuit of the simplest explanations of complicated mathematical concepts is what has held my attention in teaching my entire career.'

Opening up mathematical thinking

The real power of a mathematical hook isn't in the moment it's shown, it's in what happens next. A compelling image or scenario might grab attention, but it's the conversation that follows that turns curiosity into understanding.

One of the simplest and most effective ways to begin is with the question: 'What do you notice?'

This open invitation encourages students to observe freely, without fear of being wrong. It validates their thinking and sets the stage for deeper exploration. A spiral galaxy, for example, might prompt comments about colour, movement or symmetry. From there, the teacher can gently guide the discussion toward mathematical ideas – patterns, ratios and connections to other spirals in nature.

This approach works because it builds from what students already see and know. Rather than imposing mathematical language too early, it allows concepts to emerge organically.

To support this journey, questioning can be layered progressively:

- **Start with observation:** 'What stands out to you?', 'What patterns do you see?'
- **Move into investigation:** 'How could we measure this?', 'What might change if we altered something?'
- **Introduce mathematical connections:** 'What maths might explain this?', 'Can we represent it in a diagram or equation?'
- **Apply the idea more broadly:** 'Where else could this be useful?', 'How might this help us solve a real-world problem?'

This kind of scaffolding helps students move from surface-level noticing to deeper mathematical reasoning. It also gives teachers flexibility – allowing them to respond to student ideas in real time, rather than sticking rigidly to a script.

Ultimately, hooks aren't just about grabbing attention. They're about opening a space where students feel safe to wonder, explore and make sense of the world through a mathematical lens.

> **Classroom activity: Nature hunt**
>
> A great way to embed this approach is through a simple but powerful activity:
>
> 1. Invite students to become mathematical detectives. Ask them to collect images of patterns they notice in their environment: spirals in flowers, symmetry in architecture, tessellations in tiles or fractals in trees. These can come from their homes, walks to school or even online searches.

2 Back in the classroom, create a gallery of their findings. Encourage students to explain the mathematical ideas they see – whether it's Fibonacci sequences, geometric shapes or ratios. This turns passive observation into active exploration and helps students realise that maths isn't confined to textbooks – it's everywhere.

Hooks in action across the curriculum

Mathematical hooks can bring energy and relevance to every strand of the curriculum. Whether you're introducing algebra, geometry or statistics, the right hook can shift a lesson from abstract to engaging – especially when it connects to something students already find interesting or familiar.

In **algebra**, hooks work best when they're rooted in real-world decision-making. For example, comparing mobile phone contracts – each with different monthly costs, data allowances and call charges – naturally leads students to think in terms of variables, equations and optimisation. Similarly, exploring speed cameras or energy bills helps students see how algebra underpins everyday systems.

Geometry comes alive when students step outside the textbook. Analysing local buildings, bridges or even playground structures reveals geometric principles in action – angles, symmetry and structural design. Photography and visual art also offer rich opportunities: students can explore perspective, proportion and composition, discovering how geometry shapes the way we see and create.

In **statistics and probability**, hooks often come from students' own interests. Investigating follower growth on social media, analysing sports performance data or exploring the chances of winning in a favourite video game all provide meaningful contexts. These examples help students understand data not just as numbers, but as stories and strategies.

Here are a few more examples that work well across topics:

- **balancing equations** using physical scales and mystery weights
- **Fibonacci sequences** in sunflower spirals and pine cones
- **golden ratio** in flower petals and architecture
- **logarithmic spirals** in nautilus shells
- **fractals** in coastlines, trees and mountain ranges
- **Islamic geometric art** to explore tessellation and symmetry
- **optical illusions** that challenge assumptions about space and dimension

- **gaming algorithms** and 3D coordinate systems
- **Olympic records** and performance modelling
- **cryptocurrency and blockchain** as modern applications of mathematical logic.

These examples aren't just engaging, they're gateways. They help students see maths as a way of thinking that applies across disciplines, interests, and everyday life.

Figure 8.1 Counting the spirals of seeds in a sunflower head will generate Fibonacci numbers.

Figure 8.2 Tessellation can be seen in Moroccan tiling patterns.

Figure 8.3 Geometric optical illusions challenge our assumptions about shape and space.

Once students begin noticing patterns and asking questions, the next step is to open up space for dialogue. This is where mathematical thinking starts to take shape – not through formal instruction, but through shared exploration.

By building on student observations and gently guiding the conversation toward mathematical ideas, teachers create a space where learning feels collaborative and exploratory. It's not about having the right answer – it's about asking the right questions.

Creating your own mathematical hooks

While ready-made hooks are useful, some of the most powerful ones come from your own classroom, tailored to your students' interests, local context and lived experiences. Creating your own hooks doesn't require elaborate resources. It starts with noticing what your students care about and finding the maths within it.

Local connections are a great place to begin. Investigate traffic patterns near school, compare housing costs in the area or explore environmental data from local parks. These real-world contexts offer rich opportunities for mathematical thinking, whether it's analysing trends, calculating averages or modelling change.

School-based investigations can be just as effective. Students might measure classroom dimensions, analyse energy usage or interpret survey results from their peers. These activities make maths feel purposeful and grounded in their everyday environment.

To make hooks actually click, it helps to know what your students are interested in. Regular surveys about hobbies, digital habits and current concerns can guide your hook selection. If your class is into gaming, explore probability and algorithms. If they're passionate about music or fashion, look at patterns, ratios and design principles. And don't forget that your students can be hook creators too.

Encourage them to bring in examples from their own lives: a photo of a patterned tile, a screenshot from a game or a question about something they've noticed. When students generate the hook, they're already halfway into the maths.

> **Teaching tip: Build a hook collection**
>
> Start collecting hooks that work well with your students. Organise them by topic, difficulty level and interest area. Make notes about which ones sparked the best discussions or led to unexpected insights. Over time, you'll build a personalised resource that grows with your teaching practice.

Digital hooks and interactive possibilities

Technology opens up new dimensions for mathematical hooks. With the right tools, students can explore concepts dynamically, interact with real-time data, and see maths in action across digital platforms they already use.

- Interactive visualisation tools like GeoGebra (see Further Reading and Resources) allow students to manipulate variables and instantly see the effects. Whether they're exploring transformations, graphing equations or modelling geometric relationships, these tools make abstract ideas visible and responsive.

- Online graphing platforms and simulation software also offer rich opportunities. Students can investigate population growth, epidemic spread or financial trends, watching how mathematical models behave under different conditions. These experiences help bridge the gap between theory and application.

- Real-time data adds another layer of relevance. Weather patterns, stock prices, transport schedules – these are all sources of live data that students can analyse statistically. They can spot trends, make predictions and test hypotheses using information that feels current and meaningful.

- Social media platforms, too, are full of mathematical hooks. Students can explore how algorithms determine what content they see, how engagement rates are calculated or how data privacy is protected through encryption. These investigations show that maths isn't just behind the scenes – it's shaping their digital experience.

By combining digital tools with progressive questioning, teachers can guide students from curiosity to insight:

- 'What do you notice in this graph?'
- 'What happens if we change this variable?'
- 'What mathematical ideas are at play here?'
- 'Where else might this apply?'

Questions like these help students move from passive interaction to active reasoning and using technology to explore and understand.

Making hooks work for everyone

One of the most powerful things about mathematical hooks is their flexibility. With thoughtful choices, they can open up maths to a wide range of learners – offering multiple ways to engage, explore and make sense of ideas.

Some students respond strongly to visual prompts: striking images, colour-coded diagrams or geometric patterns that reveal structure at a glance. Others find their way in through conversation – talking about what they notice, sharing ideas and building understanding together. For some, it's the physical experience that matters: constructing models, acting out scenarios or using tools to explore balance and proportion.

Hooks can also be adapted to support students with additional needs. Multi-sensory formats, simplified visuals and concrete examples help make abstract ideas more accessible. Familiar contexts and scaffolded questioning allow students to engage deeply without being overwhelmed. For students learning English, visual and experiential hooks can reduce language barriers. Patterns, shapes and number sequences often speak across cultures. Collaborative exploration supports both mathematical thinking and language development.

The aim isn't to match students to fixed categories but to offer varied, inclusive ways into the maths. When we do that, we create a classroom where everyone has something to notice, something to say and something to discover.

Using hooks to understand student thinking

Mathematical hooks offer valuable insight into how students think, what they notice and how they approach problems. When used intentionally, hooks can support both informal and structured assessment.

At the diagnostic level, hooks help reveal what students bring to the table. Which images or scenarios capture their attention? What kinds of patterns do they spot? What questions do they ask? These responses give teachers a window into students' interests, prior knowledge and ways of seeing the world mathematically.

During lessons, hooks also support formative assessment. Listening to how students contribute to discussions – what they notice, how they explain, where they get stuck – can tell you a lot about their confidence, reasoning and conceptual understanding. Watching how they investigate a hook, whether through measurement, modelling or comparison, gives insight into their problem-solving strategies and persistence.

And perhaps most importantly, hooks reveal how students make connections. When they link a visual pattern to a mathematical concept, or apply an idea from one context to another, they're showing that the learning is sticking – and growing.

Assessment through hooks isn't about ticking boxes. It's about noticing what students notice, and using that to guide next steps. It's about seeing curiosity as a form of understanding, and recognising that sometimes the best evidence of learning is a really good question.

Culturally responsive hook design

Mathematics is often seen as universal – but the way it's taught, explored and understood is shaped by culture. When we choose hooks that reflect the diversity of our students' backgrounds, we help them see that maths isn't just something invented elsewhere – it's something they're already connected to.

This might mean drawing on global mathematical practices, from ancient number systems to architectural designs rooted in symmetry and proportion. It might mean exploring patterns found in textiles, music or art from different cultures. These examples don't just enrich the curriculum – they show students that mathematical thinking exists across time, place and tradition.

Hooks can also reflect local cultural experiences. Whether it's analysing data from the community, exploring regional geography or investigating everyday patterns in students' homes and routines, these connections help make maths feel relevant and grounded.

It's important, too, to avoid assumptions. Not every student will connect with a cultural example in the same way, and not every hook needs to be tied to identity. What matters is that students feel invited to bring their own perspectives – and that those perspectives are valued.

Encouraging students to share mathematical patterns they've noticed in their own lives, families or heritage can be a powerful way to build connection. It turns the classroom into a space where multiple ways of seeing and reasoning are welcomed.

Building a hook-rich mathematical environment

When mathematical hooks become part of the everyday classroom experience – not just occasional surprises – they help shift how students see maths. Curiosity becomes a habit. Patterns become something to look for. And mathematical thinking becomes something students feel part of, not something done to them.

This starts with the physical environment. Classrooms that display compelling images, student discoveries and mathematical patterns invite students to keep noticing. A photo of a spiral, a tessellation from a local building or a student's own sketch of a pattern they spotted on the way to school signal that maths is something to explore, not just complete. Discovery stations or investigation corners can offer space for independent exploration. A set of objects to measure, a puzzle to solve, or a visual to interpret gives students the chance to engage with maths on their own terms.

But it's not just about displays, it's about routines. A 'hook of the week' can introduce a new image, question or scenario that sparks discussion. Students might be invited to bring in their own hooks, or to vote on which one they'd like to explore further. These routines build a sense of shared ownership and curiosity. Cross-curricular connections also help. Collaborating with colleagues in art, science, geography or design can reveal unexpected mathematical links – and show students that maths doesn't live in isolation.

Over time, these small shifts create a classroom culture where noticing, wondering and exploring are part of the norm. And in that kind of environment, mathematical hooks don't just grab attention – they help shape identity.

Confidence with hooks

For many teachers, the idea of using mathematical hooks sounds exciting but also daunting. What if students ask questions you weren't expecting? What if the maths feels hard to explain on the spot?

The truth is, you don't need to have all the answers. Hooks aren't about delivering perfect explanations – they're about opening up space for shared exploration. If you find a hook genuinely interesting, your enthusiasm will carry the moment. Students respond to authenticity far more than polish.

> **Teacher tip: Start small**
>
> Choose one or two hooks that you find compelling and build a few open-ended questions around them. Let students lead the discussion. Notice what they notice. Follow their thinking. You're not expected to map out every possible direction, just to be curious alongside them.

Confidence also grows through collaboration. Sharing hooks with colleagues, swapping ideas and reflecting on what worked (and what didn't) helps build a collective toolkit. Over time, you'll find hooks that work for your students and with your teaching style.

Professional development can support this too. Conferences, online communities and subject networks often showcase hook-based teaching in action. Seeing how others use hooks to spark discussion and deepen understanding can be both inspiring and practical.

And remember: you're not trying to trick students into liking maths. You're helping them see that mathematical thinking already exists in the things they care about.

The long-term impact of mathematical hooks

When mathematical hooks become part of everyday classroom life, their influence builds gradually. Over time, they help students shift how they see maths – and how they see themselves within it.

Students begin to develop a sense of mathematical identity. They're not just completing exercises; they're noticing patterns, asking questions and thinking in ways that feel purposeful. They start spotting connections in places they hadn't before – nature, design, conversations, even their own routines.

Curiosity becomes part of how they approach the world. The more students encounter varied and engaging hooks, the more they begin to look for the maths in things they already care about. They ask better questions, take more ownership of their learning and start to see maths as something they do, not just something they're taught.

Confidence grows too. When students contribute ideas, share observations and make discoveries, they build positive associations with maths. For those who've felt excluded or unsure, these moments can be transformative. Hooks help build a sense of community. When students explore ideas together, when their thinking is valued, and when curiosity is encouraged, the classroom becomes a space where mathematical thinking is shared and celebrated. You'll start to hear students say things like: 'I never used to notice patterns and maths around me. Now I see it everywhere – and it's actually quite cool' and 'My friends ask me about maths stuff now because they know I find it interesting. It's weird being the "maths person" in my group!'

These shifts take time. But with consistent use of hooks and a classroom culture that supports noticing, wondering and exploring, they happen. And when they do, students carry mathematical thinking with them – into other subjects, into their communities, and into their futures.

Adapting to your setting

- **GCSE classrooms:** Hooks can help make abstract concepts more concrete. A compelling image or scenario at the start of a topic can spark interest and provide a reference point throughout the unit. Hooks also help maintain engagement during longer sequences of learning, offering moments of curiosity and connection.
- **Resit students:** Hooks can be especially powerful here. Many of these learners carry negative associations with maths, so the goal is to create new, positive experiences. Hooks that connect to beauty, creativity or everyday relevance – like patterns in nature or design in architecture – can help shift the narrative from 'I can't do this' to 'This is actually quite interesting.'
- **Vocational support contexts:** Hooks work best when they link directly to students' career interests. Whether it's construction, health care, digital media or business, there are mathematical ideas embedded in the work students want to do. Hooks that highlight these connections show that maths isn't just academic – it's practical, useful and already part of their world.
- **One-to-one intervention:** One-to-one contexts offer a chance to personalise hooks even further. If a student loves gaming, explore probability and algorithms. If they're into fashion, look at ratios and patterns. These tailored connections can help rebuild confidence and make maths feel more accessible.
- **SEND:** Hooks can be adapted to individual needs while still maintaining mathematical integrity. Multi-sensory formats, familiar contexts and scaffolded questioning help ensure that all students can engage meaningfully.

Key research points

- Swain, J. and Swan, M. (2007) *Thinking through mathematics: research report – Eight principles for effective teaching*.
    - Key takeaway: Rich, collaborative tasks promote discussion and communication, encourage originality and invention, are enjoyable and contain the opportunity for surprise.
    - Use it: Use hooks as opportunities to promote these principles
- GeoGebra classroom
    - Key takeaway: Dynamic mathematics software with interactive and engaging tasks for students at all levels.
    - Use it: Explore a few GeoGebra applets and see how they can be used.
- The Mathematical Association
    - Key takeaway: Hooks contained on the padlet are used to spark mathematical discussion or lead into a topic.
    - Use it: Explore the range of hooks and start to integrate into lessons.

Reflection questions

- How do I currently spark interest in mathematical ideas?
- Which hooks might resonate most with my students?
- How can I encourage students to bring their own hooks into the classroom?
- What changes could I make to the environment or routines to support more regular use of hooks?

Next steps

- Start building a collection of hooks linked to upcoming topics and student interests.
- Practice open-ended questioning that builds from observation to insight.
- Run a quick interest survey to find out what your students are curious about.
- Create displays or routines that make hooks part of the classroom culture.
- Share ideas with colleagues and learn from what's worked in their classrooms.

Chapter 9
Tools in the Toolbox

When tools get in the way of learning

A geometry set contains tools that help us measure and make sense of the world. The word 'geometry' comes from 'geo' (Earth) and 'metry' (measure). In maths lessons, students are usually expected to bring a geometry set – typically including a ruler, a pair of compasses with a pencil, a protractor as well as a scientific calculator.

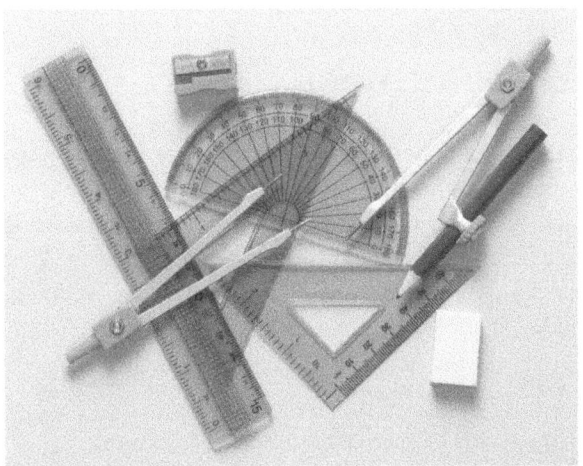

Figure 9.1 Many students find using a standard geometry set and calculator challenging.

For students lacking confidence in maths, these tools can feel like just one more hurdle. Struggling with a protractor isn't just about losing marks, it can chip away at their confidence. If compass work goes wrong, it can reinforce their belief that they 'just can't do maths.'

The pandemic made these challenges even more pronounced. Many students missed out on regular practice with geometry sets and calculators at home, leaving them feeling even less sure of themselves. Examiner reports frequently highlight poor performance with protractors, rulers, compasses and calculators. Just like a chef's knife or a mechanic's wrench, tools only work well with practice. Mastering any tool requires time, patience and support, and that journey looks different for every student.

In this chapter, we'll explore how to spot tool-related challenges, offer inclusive teaching strategies and create a classroom where every student can succeed in geometry.

> **Teaching tip: Building tool confidence**
>
> When students feel anxious about tools, it's a sign of deeper insecurities in maths. When they struggle to use a protractor or compass, they're not just wrestling with the physical tools, they're also battling their belief that they 'can't do maths.' We need to help them see tool practice as a way to build skills, not just prep for exams: 'Practice not until you get it right, but until you can't get it wrong!'

Confidence and readiness

Let's start by exploring how tool anxiety shows up in the classroom and how we can build student confidence from the ground up.

In GCSE maths assessments, students spend around three hours using calculators and four and a half hours using rulers, protractors and compasses. After each exam series, examiner reports consistently highlight common issues with tool use. Typical comments include:

- The angle for QPS was often drawn incorrectly.
- The length of the given line was measured outside of the tolerance.
- Some students did not use or show the working from their calculator.
- This question was not well answered and there were a large number of non-attempts.

These comments show *where* students struggle, but they rarely explain *why*. They don't explore the emotional or practical barriers that lead to these mistakes.

Students often express their frustration: 'In my mock exam, I spent ages trying to measure this angle and still got it wrong. Then I panicked and messed up the rest of the question. It's not fair to lose marks just because I couldn't use the protractor!' This kind of experience can quickly spiral into mathematical panic, meaning that what starts as a practical challenge becomes even more emotional evidence of failure, especially for students who already feel vulnerable.

Spotting tool challenges

Taking a moment to observe how students use their tools reveals a lot about the support they need. For example, a student struggling with compasses might have difficulty with hand coordination. Another might misalign a protractor due to visual processing differences; perhaps they've never been shown how to line up the angle with the crosshatch. Some students hold calculators awkwardly, using their thumbs to enter numbers while holding it in one hand. Others avoid reading results aloud, which can signal difficulty with decimal place value (you might hear 'twenty-one point twelve' when they mean 'twenty-one point one two').

These behaviours aren't signs of being 'bad at maths' – they're clues. They point to specific needs that can be addressed with the right support. Using rulers, protractors and compasses requires fine motor skills that ideally should be developed before GCSE. But lack of equipment, limited practice time and overlooked skill-building often mean students arrive underprepared. Some may benefit from adapted tools, such as rulers with handles or large-print protractors. Spotting these challenges early allows us to respond with empathy and practical solutions, rather than frustration.

Classroom dialogue: Introducing mathematical tools

Tool anxiety often shows up in everyday classroom conversations. Here's an example of how you might respond supportively:

Student: 'I can't use this protractor… it's fiddly and confusing.'
Teacher: 'Using tools is important, not just for exams, and not just maths tools like this.'
Student: 'When will I ever need to use this, though?'
Teacher: 'That's a great question. How do you know what you'll be doing in the future? Do you know anyone who uses tools like this in their job? I bet using an airgun in a garage would seem confusing at first too.'
Student: 'I don't know anyone who even has a protractor!'
Teacher: 'There are loads of tools you might use later on that seem confusing at first. So how do you get good at using any new tool?'

This kind of dialogue helps students reflect on their own learning and builds a bridge between classroom tools and real-world applications. You might use analogies like hair straighteners, kitchen gadgets or even gaming controllers; tools that students are familiar with and had to learn to use.

Foundational skills and practice

With confidence growing, we can now focus on the foundational skills students need to use their tools effectively.

From construction practice to tool mastery

The key to success in using the tools is supporting students to feel more confident with basic constructions. Then it's time to deepen their understanding of individual tools. This is where we shift from isolated practice to purposeful mastery – building fluency that supports wider mathematical thinking. Before diving into each tool, it's worth remembering that confidence grows through repeated, supported use. Whether it's drawing a line segment, measuring an angle or using a calculator, students need time, space and encouragement to get it right – and then keep getting it right.

Using a ruler

Measuring and drawing with a ruler may seem straightforward, but many students struggle with aligning the ruler correctly (starting from zero, not the edge), reading measurements accurately and using the correct units.

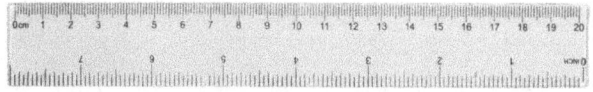

Figure 9.2 Give students plenty of practice using rulers.

These are fine motor skills that need modelling and practice. Use a visualiser to demonstrate ruler use clearly, or share an animation or YouTube clip. GeoGebra (see Further Reading and Resources) also offers interactive applets that can support this.

Ask questions about the scale on the ruler, e.g. 'What do you notice? Who has the sharpest pencil – why does this matter?' Use this for retrieval practice on millimetres, centimetres and metres and the conversions between them. Find your classroom experts in the skill and use them to support other students.

> **Teaching tip: Age-appropriate resources**
>
> Avoid Key Stage 2 resources. Choose adult or real-life examples that add relevance and meaning.

Using a protractor

Protractors come in different forms: full circles to semi-circles, some with a holding wheel at the centre. The only reason we have semi-circular protractors is so it can fit into a geometry set!

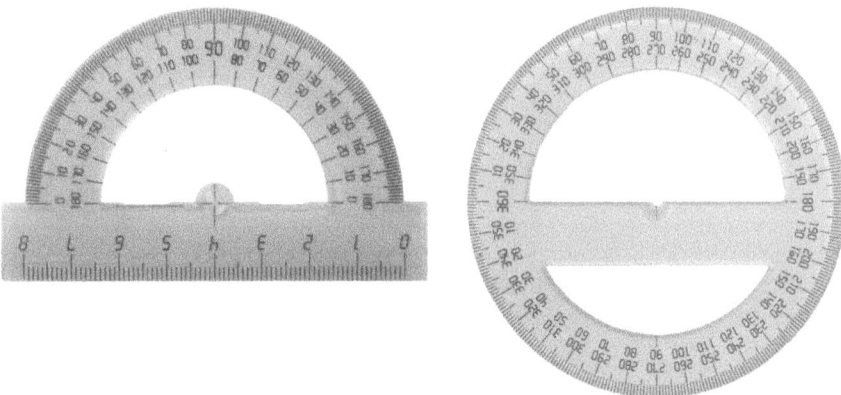

Figure 9.3 Students often find choosing the right scale on a protractor difficult.

Protractors can be tricky for students. Common challenges include: aligning the crosshair (or origin) with the angle's vertex, choosing the correct scale (inner or outer) and reading angles accurately. These difficulties are often compounded by lack of modelling. Estimation can help – encourage students to guess the angle size before measuring. This helps them choose the correct scale and builds their number sense. It can also help remind them of the correct terminology.

Tom Francome advocates using 'empty protractors' – tools without numbers – to help students focus on the concept of angle as a measure of turn (Francome, 2016). You can easily make one yourself or find printable versions online.

Using a pair of compasses

Compasses are one of the most misunderstood tools in the geometry set and often the most fiddly! First, clarify the terminology: a compass (for navigation) and a pair of compasses (for drawing) are different tools. Students often confuse the two.

The quality of the tool matters. Poorly made compasses can slip, wobble or tear the paper, making neat constructions almost impossible. Before teaching compass skills, take time to go back to basics:

- show students the different parts: the needle, legs, hinge and handle
- emphasise the importance of a short, sharp pencil
- demonstrate how to hold the compass at the top – not by the legs – and rotate it smoothly
- model how compasses work in combination with rulers and protractors to bisect lines and angles.

Common errors made when using a compass include:

- measuring the radius inaccurately
- holding the legs and pushing them around
- moving the paper instead of the compass
- using a blunt or overly long pencil.

Use a visualiser or animated clip to model correct technique. Better still, identify a confident student and let them demonstrate.

Why these skills matter

These basic construction skills are essential for later geometry work like bearings, parallel lines and circle theorems. Use retrieval practice to reinforce angle facts and tackle misconceptions early. Understanding angles as measures of turn, and using correct terms like *vertex* and *arm*, lays the groundwork for confident, accurate constructions.

Creative and gamified practice

To keep practice engaging, let's look at creative and gamified strategies that help students master tool use.

Classroom activity: Protractor instructions

Once students understand how to use a protractor, give them a chance to consolidate their learning through a creative task.

- Start with a written challenge: Ask students to produce a clear, step-by-step guide titled 'How to use a protractor', including definitions for key terms like *angle*, *vertex* and *arm*. This reinforces vocabulary and helps them reflect on the process.
- Then move into a drawing challenge. Set criteria such as:
  - a line exactly 6.2 cm long
  - an acute angle
  - a circle with a radius of 4 cm
  - three angles between 45° and 170°.

Students can incorporate these into stick-person drawings, following your instructions. This adds a playful, low-pressure way to practise tool use. They can then measure the angles in their own or each other's work. (Stick-people are simple, accessible and fun, but for students who find them too childish, offer alternatives like garden layouts, architectural sketches or Islamic art designs. The key is giving students a choice in how they demonstrate their skills.)

Use a visualiser to showcase the most accurate or imaginative examples. Drawing activities like this can settle learners, encourage precision and offer a creative route into geometry.

Classroom activity: Freehand circle challenge

Drawing circles is a gateway to constructions and a great way to build confidence with a tool that often causes anxiety. This light-hearted activity settles learners and leads naturally into accurate compass use.

1. Start with a fun warm up: challenge students to draw a perfect freehand circle.
2. Show the famous YouTube clip of Alexander Overwijk, a maths teacher who went viral for his ability to draw perfect freehand circles.
3. Let students try at the board and vote on the best attempt.

4 Follow up by reviewing key vocabulary: radius, diameter, circumference, arc, tangent, chord, sector, segment.
5 You could extend this by asking students, the next time that they have a pizza, to show these parts of the circle on it and send you a picture! Alternatively, you could label up a dartboard.

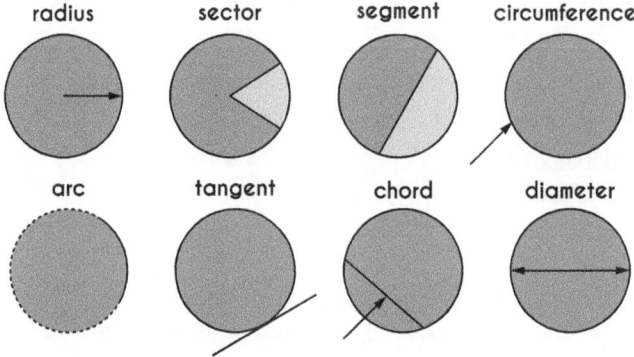

Figure 9.4 The key parts of a circle.

Transum Maths

For students who find traditional practice dull or intimidating, gamified platforms like Transum Maths (see Further Reading and Resources) offer a fresh approach. Transum provides interactive activities where students can practise measuring angles, drawing constructions and using mathematical tools in game-like formats. Students progress through levels, earn points and badges, and receive instant feedback, turning 'boring practice' into 'I want to try the next level'. The low-stakes environment helps students learn from mistakes without the pressure of permanent marks on paper.

What makes Transum particularly valuable is its simulation of real mathematical instruments. Students can practise reading protractors, using virtual rulers and working with compass constructions before handling physical tools. This builds familiarity and confidence, especially for reluctant learners.

Estimation and accuracy are built into many of these activities. Students are prompted to estimate before measuring, reinforcing number sense and helping them choose the correct scale. They also encounter tasks involving rounding, decimal places and significant figures, all key parts of the Limits of Accuracy strand in GCSE maths.

You can use Transum for homework, intervention, or in-class practice. It's flexible: you decide whether to track student progress or let them explore freely. This can reduce anxiety and encourage independent learning.

Advanced applications

Once students are comfortable with individual tools, they're ready to combine them for more advanced constructions and calculator work.

Combining skills: Advanced constructions

Once students are confident using individual tools, they're ready to combine those skills for more complex constructions. This is where everything – ruler, compass, protractor – comes together, and where fluency really starts to show. Here are three key constructions that build on earlier learning:

- Line bisection: Use compasses to draw arcs above and below the line from each end, then connect the points where the arcs intersect.

- Angle bisection: Place the compass on the angle's vertex and draw an arc across both arms. From each point where the arc crosses, draw intersecting arcs and connect the intersection to the vertex.

- Triangle construction requires accurate use of all tools – drawing and measuring line segments, angles and arcs.

> **Hear from the expert: Clarissa Grandi, Artful Maths**
>
> 'Mathematical artmaking is a fantastic way to help build visuo-spatial skills and manual dexterity, skills which are intrinsic to geometric fluency in later mathematics. Research by exam boards has shown that the geometry and measures questions are those most often left entirely unattempted in GCSE mathematics exams. This is an indication that our students are not confident in their geometry, nor with using their construction and measuring tools: their rulers, protractors and compasses.'

Confidence builder: Teaching mathematical tools

- If you're feeling unsure about teaching tool-based skills, start by building your own confidence. Practise the basics, e.g. measuring line segments and angles, drawing circles with a given radius or diameter, using your calculator fluently.
- Take a look at Artful Maths and the beautiful artwork created there, which you can recreate.
- You can find simple, step-by-step YouTube clips to support your teaching – search for 'basic geometric constructions'. Practise these yourself first; your confidence will transfer directly to your students.
- Create a simple cheat sheet with steps for each skill. Source clear, scaffolded resources – like instructables or short clips – to support students who need extra help.
- Be honest with your class. Say something like, 'I'm learning new ways to use these tools too – let's explore them together.' This models a growth mindset and helps students see learning as a shared journey.

These constructions lay the foundation for topics like loci, circle theorems, bearings and trigonometry, some of which appear on the higher tier. They also reinforce spatial reasoning and precision, skills that benefit students across all subjects. This shift from isolated tool use to integrated construction work is a key milestone where students begin to see geometry as a system, not just a set of steps.

Calculator mastery

Calculators are essential tools at GCSE but many students lack confidence using them. A quick glance at how a student holds and uses their calculator can tell you a lot:

- Do they hold it in one hand and type with their thumb, like a phone?
- Do they avoid reading the answer aloud?
- Do they hesitate before pressing keys?

These behaviours often signal unfamiliarity or anxiety. As Craig Barton says, 'the students who most need a calculator are usually the least proficient in using one' (Barton, 2025).

A calculator is a gadget. It will only do what you ask it to do. It's capable of many advanced calculations, which can make the number of buttons and options feel overwhelming. But students only need familiarity with a small number of features at GCSE level.

> **Teaching tip: Build calculator confidence**
>
> - Make calculator use a regular part of lessons, not just something saved for exam prep. This helps students practise key functions, check their work independently and reduce cognitive load on procedural tasks.
> - Encourage them to explore their calculator's features and get comfortable with its layout. If possible, get all students to use the same model to avoid confusion.
> - Remind them that 5 per cent of calculators run out of battery during the exam, so they should make sure theirs is either solar-powered or has a fresh battery in it.
> - There are a range of adaptive calculators for partially sighted and other different needs. They are usually pricey but well worth exploring the manufacturers website.

Essential calculator skills

Focus on the functions students actually need for GCSE:

- Basic operations: +, −, ×, ÷
- Powers and roots: x^2, x^3, $\sqrt{}$, $\sqrt[3]{}$
- Fractions: a/b button
- Percentages: % button (though multipliers are often more reliable)
- Memory: STO and RCL
- Brackets: ( ) for order of operations
- Trigonometry: sin, cos, tan (ensure degree mode is on)
- Time calculations: hours, minutes, seconds.

Practise these yourself – students quickly pick up on teacher uncertainty.

Common mistakes to watch for

Students often avoid using calculators even when allowed. For example:

- attempting 17% of 25 manually
- adding fractions like $\frac{2}{3} + \frac{1}{5}$ by hand

- using build-up methods (10% + 1% + 2%) instead of a multiplier (e.g. × 0.13). Students who show this working on a calculator paper will not gain the marks.

In calculator papers, marks are often awarded for correct calculator use, not just the answer, so we need to encourage students to use the tool confidently and appropriately. As Craig Barton says, 'just give them the calculator!'

Practical teaching strategies

Supporting tool mastery also means managing equipment and modelling techniques effectively in the classroom.

Script box: Getting to grips with mathematical tools

When a student says: 'I can't use a compass to draw a circle or arc marks. I've never been able to do it.'

- Say this: 'That's because you haven't practised enough. How do you get good at anything? Football, drawing, cooking, FIFA? What if you bought a new phone – how would learn to use it?'
- Not this: 'You need to be able to do this for the exam… Let's go over it again.'
- Follow-up: 'What advice would you give someone else who is struggling to use these tools? Could you write down some instructions? Imagine you're teaching your little sister to do this, or your Gran.'

Managing classroom equipment

One of the most common barriers to tool mastery is simple: students don't bring the equipment. Whether it's a missing ruler, a blunt pencil or no calculator at all, these gaps can derail a lesson.

Schools may not have the budget to provide high-quality geometry sets and calculators for everyone, so it helps to have a clear classroom strategy.

> **Teaching tip: Equipment exchange**
>
> One approach I've used is an equipment exchange system. If a student forgot a tool, they could borrow mine – but only by leaving something important in return. Over the years, I've held everything from chocolate bars to a set of go-kart wheels on my desk! It became a light-hearted but effective way to reinforce responsibility.

At the start of the year, set expectations clearly. Regular checks early on help build habits. Encourage students to source their own kits from charity shops or online marketplaces: geometry sets and revision guides are often available cheaply. Keep a small classroom supply for emergencies, and make sure students know it's there. The goal is to remove barriers, not add pressure.

> **Teaching tip: Using a visualiser effectively**
>
> A visualiser is one of the most versatile tools in your classroom toolkit – especially when teaching physical skills like constructions or calculator use. It allows students to follow your steps in real time, watching how tools are used with precision and care.
>
> Visualisers are relatively inexpensive (starting around £50) and easy to set up. Once in place, they can be used to:
>
> - demonstrate constructions step by step
> - show live work rather than animations
> - model calculator use without needing an emulator
> - display student work to the whole class
> - showcase layout, presentation and working
> - record tutorials for future use
> - create stop-motion animations for cross-curricular projects.

When students see real hands using real tools, it builds trust and clarity. It's not just about showing, it's about modelling confidence and technique. Encourage them to become experts too, by letting them lead demonstrations using the visualiser, reinforcing their skills and boosting classroom collaboration.

Assessment language

Understanding the language of assessment is just as important as mastering the tools themselves. Command words like *sketch*, *draw*, *estimate* and *work out* each carry specific expectations and students often miss marks simply because they misinterpret what's being asked. You'll explore this in more detail in Chapter 10, but it's worth introducing the idea early.

Use strategies like Frayer Models (see Chapter 5) to help students unpack key terms. These visual organisers support vocabulary development and clarify what each word means in practice. For example, *estimate* might involve rounding or approximation, while *work out* signals a need for calculation and precision. Helping students spot these differences builds confidence and exam readiness.

Adapting to your setting

- **GCSE classrooms:** Link basic tool skills (e.g. drawing line segments and circles, and measuring angles) to more advanced topics like bearings, constructions and circle theorems. Reinforce connections to other subjects such as science and art, where precision and spatial reasoning are equally important.
- **Resit students:** Engagement is key. Use creative tasks like stick-person drawings or Mondrian-inspired artwork to make geometry feel fresh and accessible. Gamified platforms like Transum Maths can help students practise protractor and calculator skills in a low-pressure, motivating way.
- **Vocational support contexts:** In these contexts you need to make the learning relevant. Use examples from trades such as construction, architecture and landscape design to show how these tools are used in real-world planning and measurement. Share examiner report findings with colleagues across departments to build a consistent, cross-curricular approach.
- **One-to-one intervention:** Start with concrete examples. Use images, discussion prompts or even a 'geometry hunt' around the school to help students spot shapes and tools in everyday life. This builds familiarity and confidence in a more personal, exploratory way.

Key research points

- Awarding Bodies: Examiner Reports
  - Key takeaway: Your exam board produces analysis of student performance in every exam series. These give valuable insights.
  - Use it: Download and read the latest series of Examiner Reports. Highlight certain phrases to use in your classroom.

- Craig Barton: Just give them a calculator![3]
  - Key takeaway: Allow students to use the calculator whenever they want.
  - Use it: Sign up for all of the EEDI newsletter from Craig. They are well worth a read.

Reflection questions

- Which motor skills do you feel confident teaching?
- Which ones do you need to practise: bisecting an angle, drawing an equilateral triangle, using a compass accurately?
- Who are your classroom experts? How could you empower them to support others, perhaps by leading a demo or creating instruction sheets?

Next steps

- Observe how students use their tools. What difficulties do you notice?
- Use your visualiser to model skills – or invite a student expert to do so.
- Create regular practice opportunities: stick-person drawings, Mondrian-inspired art, garden layouts or cake designs.
- Develop a cross-departmental approach to tool use. Share examiner report findings and align strategies across subjects.

Part Four

Achieving Success

Chapter 10
Solving the Problem with Problem Solving

From 'I don't know where to start' to 'I can figure this out'

'I look at word problems and my mind goes blank. There are so many words and numbers mixed together, and I don't know what I'm supposed to do with them. I just skip to the next question because I know I'll get it wrong anyway.'

This student has articulated the most common barrier to mathematical problem solving: the paralysis that comes from not knowing where to begin. She has the mathematical knowledge needed to solve many problems, but the transition from recognising a problem to developing a solution strategy feels impossible.

This isn't about mathematical ability; it's about problem-solving confidence and systematic approaches to unfamiliar challenges. True problem solving requires working with uncertainty, developing strategies through trial and exploration, and persisting through confusion toward understanding. Yet many students have learned to avoid this productive struggle, seeking immediate clarity rather than engaging with the problem-solving process.

The difficulty intensifies for students who've experienced repeated problem-solving failures. They've learned to recognise problems as threats to their mathematical confidence rather than opportunities for mathematical thinking. When they encounter unfamiliar problems, their instinct is protection rather than exploration.

This chapter explores how to transform problem solving from a source of anxiety into a pathway to mathematical confidence, building systematic approaches that help students move from 'I don't know where to start' to 'I can figure this out' through patient, supported practice with genuine mathematical challenges.

The problem-solving paradox

The main challenge with problem solving is that students need to face uncertainty and struggle to build their skills, but these experiences can feel uncomfortable and frightening. Students who expect immediate clarity often find it hard to deal with the uncertainties of real maths problems. Traditional maths education usually focuses on clear procedures and algorithms to find solutions. Students learn to identify problem types and use specific methods, which helps them become good at calculations but limits their ability to solve different problems. So when they face new exercises that don't resemble what they've practised, they often don't know how to start.

> **Hear from the expert: Colin Foster, Professor of Mathematics Education**
>
> 'If you know how to solve the problem before you start, then it's an exercise, not a problem. Just giving students opportunities to try solving problems is not teaching them problem solving. Helping students solve a problem today doesn't necessarily make them better problem solvers in the future.'
>
> Colin also reminds us that good problem solvers have solid maths foundations and that problem solving difficulty is often really fluency difficulty.

How often do your students come across math problems without an obvious solution? These situations encourage them to think creatively and come up with original ideas. George Polya, a key figure in problem solving, suggested four important steps to help solve these problems: first, understand the problem; second, make a plan; third, carry out the plan; and finally, check the solution to ensure it's correct (Polya, 1945). These steps give structure to problem solving, while also recognising that the process can be flexible and non-linear.

However, many students skip directly from reading a problem to attempting calculations, missing the crucial understanding and planning phases that make problem solving systematic rather than random. They need explicit instruction in problem-solving strategies that provide structure without removing the productive challenge.

> **Student voice: The emotional reality of problem solving**
>
> Many students experience a deep sense of anxiety when faced with unfamiliar mathematical problems. One Year 10 student described how she often panics, convinced that everyone else understands something she

> doesn't, and too embarrassed to ask for help – so she sits quietly, feeling inadequate. Another student, retaking maths, shared that while he's confident with calculations, he struggles when problems are wrapped in stories or real-life contexts. He finds himself guessing, combining numbers at random, hoping something will stick. A Year 11 student explained that even when she understands the problem, she freezes when asked to show her working, unsure how to express her thinking clearly. Chinn and Ashcroft (2017) analyses thinking styles in maths in terms of inchworms and grasshoppers, and encourages us to teach with the diversity of thinking in mind.

The emotional dimension of problem solving is as important as the cognitive dimension. Some exam boards have a term for students who take one look at a larger, wordy problem and move on...the page-turners.

Building problem-solving confidence through systematic approaches

Students need clear instruction in problem-solving strategies that provide support while encouraging mathematical thinking. These strategies should help students tackle new problems without stifling their creativity.

> **Teaching tip: Normalising the problem-solving struggle**
>
> - Teach students that feeling confused or uncertain is a normal part of problem solving. Use phrases like 'It's okay to feel stuck with this type of problem' to make them feel better about their confusion.
> - Show students your thinking process as you solve problems. Talk about your moments of confusion, mistakes and changes in strategy. This helps students see that even experienced problem solvers go through uncertainty too, instead of having all the answers right away.

Talking through your thinking aloud, especially during moments of uncertainty or when changing approaches, is a key teaching practice. It illustrates metacognition: helping students understand and manage their thinking processes. Research shows that using metacognitive strategies significantly boosts students' achievements in all subjects, with particularly strong benefits for disadvantaged learners (Education Endowment Foundation, 2018).

Visual representation strategies

Many students find problem solving easier when they can use visuals rather than relying solely on words and numbers. Visual representations often reveal the structure of a problem that isn't immediately obvious in written form.

- **Bar modelling** helps students make sense of problems involving ratios, proportions and comparisons. Drawing bars to represent quantities turns abstract relationships into something concrete and easier to manipulate.

- **Diagram drawing** supports students in visualising geometric problems, journey scenarios and spatial challenges. Even when diagrams aren't required, creating one can clarify the underlying structure. In the words of Piximaths (see Further Reading and Resources), 'if it's tricky, draw a piccy!'.

Both bar modelling and diagram drawing help students extract the maths from the words and make sense of it visually. Pete Mattock, author of *Visible Maths*, tells us that models help students make sense of the maths, helping them to find a route in (Mattock, 2019).

Classroom activity: Problem-solving strategies toolkit

Build a class collection of problem-solving strategies through collaborative exploration:

- Strategy 1: Work backwards – start with the answer and figure out how to get there.
- Strategy 2: Make a table – organise information systematically to spot patterns.
- Strategy 3: Look for patterns – find regularities that suggest general approaches.
- Strategy 4: Simplify the problem – try easier versions first, then build complexity.
- Strategy 5: Guess and check – make educated guesses and refine based on results.
- Strategy 6: Draw a picture – create visual representations of problem situations.

Students contribute examples of when each strategy works well, building collective problem-solving knowledge while developing individual strategic thinking.

Scaffolding problem-solving development

Build students' confidence and strategic thinking through graduated exposure to problem-solving challenges. This progression begins with guided problem solving, where you model your thinking aloud – rather than simply seeing the final answer, students observe the full process of mathematical reasoning. As students grow more comfortable, collaborative problem solving offers the next step. Working in pairs or small groups allows them to share the cognitive load, test out strategies together, and build confidence through shared success. These interactions also help students articulate their thinking and learn from different approaches. Finally, they move towards independent problem solving, applying strategies on their own with increasing confidence. Worked examples will support this scaffolded approach (Pritchard, 2022).

Script box: Supporting stuck students

When a student says: 'I don't know what to do. I've read it three times and I still don't understand.'

- Say this: 'That's completely normal with this type of problem. Let's start by identifying what the problem is asking you to find. Don't worry about how to solve it yet – just focus on what question you need to answer.'
- Not this: 'Just try something and see what happens.'
- Follow-up: 'Now that we know what we're looking for, what information has the problem given us? Let's gather all the pieces before we worry about putting them together.'

This approach breaks problem solving into manageable steps while maintaining the student's ownership of the thinking process.

Addressing the language barrier

Many students struggle with problem solving not because the maths is too difficult, but because the language used in word problems can be overwhelming. Extracting mathematical meaning from verbal contexts requires significant language processing, which can be especially challenging for students with reading difficulties or those learning English as an additional language. To support these learners, decoding strategies can be taught to help them identify key mathematical vocabulary, separate essential information from decorative detail, and translate verbal descriptions into mathematical representations. Buddying up an EAL student with a student with weaker maths skills but good English ability is a great strategy to employ.

Familiarity with context also plays a crucial role, as students are more likely to engage with problems that reflect their own experiences than those requiring cultural knowledge they may not have. This doesn't mean avoiding unfamiliar contexts altogether, but rather ensuring a balance that includes problems students can relate to. For EAL learners, additional support might include offering problems in heritage languages where possible, using visual aids to reduce reliance on text, encouraging collaborative work where peers can help translate, and explicitly teaching mathematical vocabulary rather than assuming prior understanding.

Classroom dialogue: Working through problem-solving uncertainty

Teacher: 'I can see some of you are stuck – and that's okay. This kind of problem is meant to make us think, not just plug in a method we already know.'

Student A: 'But I don't even know where to start; I've never done this before!'

Teacher: 'Well, the context might be new, but the maths underneath it is familiar. Let's figure out what the question is really asking.'

Student B: 'Are we supposed to know how to do this already?'

Teacher: 'Nope. This is one of those problems where we need to pull together different bits of what we know. That's what makes it proper problem solving, not just an exercise.'

Student C: 'But what if I get it wrong?'

Teacher: 'Getting it wrong is part of the process. Right now, I'm more interested in how you're thinking than whether the final answer is correct.'

This model dialogue shows how you can encourage problem solving as a way to explore ideas instead of just getting the right answer, which helps reduce anxiety and increases engagement. It's also important to remember that problem-solving skills are what employers look for. If you can identify a problem and suggest a solution, you become a valuable asset.

Building persistence and tenacity

Experiences that help students solve problems while offering support build their mathematical resilience, meaning they are more likely to keep trying even when maths gets tough. It helps them stay confident when they feel unsure, and gain confidence through real success instead of easy answers. A growth mindset develops when students see improvement comes from effort and learning new strategies instead of thinking their maths ability is fixed, and problem solving gives students a chance to connect their progress to their hard work.

Assessment methods that support problem solving are essential, especially when traditional tests tend to focus on correct answers while overlooking how students think. Effective problem-solving assessment values reasoning, strategy use and persistence – not just calculations. Process-focused rubrics help evaluate how students approach problems, giving credit for logical thinking, appropriate strategy choices and clear explanations. Other useful approaches include giving students a solution and asking whether it's correct, or using spoof assessments (see Chapter 6) where they're told the answer they see is wrong and must explain why. Peer assessment also plays a valuable role, helping students develop evaluation skills and mathematical communication by recognising and appreciating different ways to solve the same problem.

Confidence builder: Teaching problem solving when you feel uncertain

Many teachers feel uneasy with problem-solving instruction because it involves managing uncertainty and helping students struggle instead of just giving clear steps. Your role is to help students think, not to show them how to solve problems perfectly.

- Ask good questions to guide their thinking: 'What do you notice about this problem?', 'What strategies might work here?' or 'How can you check if your answer makes sense?' These questions help students reason and keep them engaged in the problem-solving process.
- Be open about your own problem-solving methods. When working through problems with students, share your thoughts, including your doubts, any changes in your strategies and reflections on what worked. This shows real mathematical thinking instead of pretending to be an expert.

Problem solving across different mathematical contexts

Different areas of mathematics offer unique opportunities for solving problems, each with its own challenges and strategies.

- Numerical problems often involve finding patterns in number sequences, optimising solutions or exploring mathematical relationships. These problems usually require systematic testing and pattern recognition.

- Geometric problems focus on visualisation, spatial reasoning and measurement. Students must develop both analytical skills and intuitive approaches to tackle these spatial challenges.

- Algebraic problems involve manipulating symbols, solving equations and reasoning abstractly. Students should connect algebraic methods to real-life situations instead of treating them as unrelated skills.

- Statistical problems include interpreting data, reasoning about probability and making informed conclusions. These problems involve both mathematical calculations and logical thinking about uncertainty.

Problem solving is the thread that runs through every area of mathematics – whether students are spotting patterns, visualising shapes, solving equations or interpreting data. But helping them become confident problem solvers isn't just about teaching techniques; it's about creating the conditions where thinking, experimenting and persevering are part of everyday learning.

This means building a classroom culture where problem solving is expected, supported and valued. The physical space matters – students need room to collaborate, access to visual tools, and environments that invite extended thinking. Equally important are the social norms: where struggle is normal, diverse approaches are welcomed, and students feel safe to take risks. Time is a factor, too. Problem solving shouldn't be squeezed into the last few minutes of a lesson. Starting with a rich, wordy problem can signal that deep thinking is central, not an afterthought.

Of course, this is challenging, especially with resit and FE students who have low confidence and negative experiences of maths. Shifting mindsets takes time, patience and a series of small, meaningful wins. But when students begin to see themselves as capable of tackling unfamiliar problems, the impact is transformative. They develop habits of thinking that help them navigate uncertainty, solve real-world challenges and approach future learning with greater confidence.

The shift from 'I don't know where to start' to 'I can figure this out' is one of the most powerful outcomes of mathematical education. It's not just about solving problems, it's about building students who are resilient, resourceful and ready for whatever comes next.

Adapting to your setting

- **GCSE classrooms:** Prepare students for exams by providing real problem-solving experiences. Show how solving problems helps with unfamiliar exam questions.
- **Resit students:** Reduce anxiety about new problems by teaching systematic approaches.
- **Vocational support contexts:** Use real workplace problems that need maths thinking. Show how problem-solving skills apply in professional settings.
- **One-to-one Intervention:** Offer focused support for students who feel anxious about solving problems. Build their confidence with step-by-step challenges and strategy development.
- **Adult learners:** Link problem solving to real-life issues and career growth. Show how maths thinking helps with different decisions and responsibilities.

Key research points

- Colin Foster: Problem-Solving in Mathematics Education (2013)
    - Key takeaway: Foster argues that if students already know how to solve a problem before they begin, it's not truly a problem – it's an exercise. Real problem solving involves uncertainty, exploration and strategic thinking.
    - How to use it: Design tasks that require students to think creatively and develop their own approaches, rather than simply applying memorised procedures.
- George Polya: *How to Solve It: A New Aspect of Mathematical Method* (1945)
    - Key takeaway: Polya's framework outlines four phases of problem solving: understanding the problem, devising a plan, carrying out the plan and looking back. These phases help structure mathematical thinking and support strategic development.
    - How to use it: Teach problem solving as a systematic process. Model each phase explicitly and encourage students to reflect on their strategies and outcomes.
- Carol Dweck et al.: *Growth Mindset and Mathematics Achievement* (2016)
    - Key takeaway: Students who believe mathematical ability can be developed through effort and strategy show greater persistence and success in problem solving than those who view ability as fixed.
    - How to use it: Emphasise effort, strategy development and progress over time. Use feedback that reinforces growth and encourages students to see mistakes as part of learning.

Reflection questions

- How do I currently support students who feel overwhelmed by unfamiliar problems? Do my classroom routines, language and modelling help students feel safe to struggle? Do I explicitly teach that confusion is part of learning?
- Which students might benefit most from more structured problem-solving instruction? What scaffolds could help build confidence for learners who often skip word problems, freeze when asked to explain their thinking or rely heavily on memorised methods?
- How can I create a classroom culture that encourages mathematical risk-taking? How do I respond to mistakes and celebrate different approaches? Do students feel comfortable sharing partial or uncertain thinking?
- What assessment strategies could I use to value problem-solving thinking? Explore ways to assess process over product – such as using rubrics that reward reasoning, asking students to critique solutions, or incorporating peer feedback on strategy use.

Next steps

- Introduce structured strategies that support thinking without removing challenge.
- Model your own problem-solving process – including uncertainty and reflection.
- Sequence tasks from supported to independent to build confidence gradually.
- Use assessments that reward reasoning and strategy, not just correct answers.
- Foster a classroom culture where persistence and creative thinking are valued.

Chapter 11
From Exam Panic to Exam Power

Transforming exam anxiety into mathematical confidence

The exam hall falls silent as 200 students turn over their papers. Within minutes, a familiar pattern emerges: some students dive in confidently, others sit frozen, and many begin working frantically without reading questions properly. In the corner, a student stares at question one, a straightforward percentage calculation he has practised hundreds of times, but his mind has gone completely blank.

This scene plays out across the country every summer. Students who demonstrate solid mathematical understanding in classroom discussions suddenly can't access their knowledge under pressure. Others lose crucial marks not through mathematical misunderstanding but through copying errors, unclear working or missing out questions they could easily answer.

The cruellest irony is that students who've worked hardest to overcome mathematical difficulties often struggle most with exam anxiety. After months or years of building confidence, a few pressured hours can undo all that progress. This student isn't unusual; they represent thousands of pupils whose exam performance fails to reflect their actual mathematical capability.

For students retaking exams, the pressure feels extremely high. They may lose up to 10 marks because of technique-related problems. These marks could be crucial for achieving the Grade 4 they need for their plans. And then there's the exam setting itself. Imagine being one of over a thousand students sitting the same paper in the same hall. It's no wonder anxiety spikes. For resit students especially, this can be overwhelming. It's not unusual for these cohorts to be huge, with many needing extra time, a reader or a scribe. The logistics are intense, and for students already feeling vulnerable, the scale of it can make things worse. We need to help them manage that; not just the maths, but the whole experience.

This chapter changes the story about exam failure. We'll look at how failing an exam often has little to do with maths skills and more to do with problems in technique that we can fix. Moving from exam anxiety to exam success isn't about getting rid of nerves; some anxiety can actually help performance. It's about using that energy in a focused way, with practice, to get the best possible score. This applies to everyone, regardless of their past experiences.

Understanding exam technique failure

The first step to improvement is realising that 'poor exam technique' is not a personal failing but a skills gap we can fill with the right support and practice. When I give students their marked mock papers, a common scene happens. I say, 'You've done really well, but let's see where you lost some marks.' Students often stare at their work, confused. They ask, 'Why did I put *that*, Miss?!' They aren't being dramatic; they are genuinely surprised by their mistakes.

These aren't just careless mistakes, but predictable patterns that show how mathematical knowledge, emotions and testing conditions interact. Research by Beilock and Carr shows that test anxiety can significantly reduce working memory, especially for students who usually perform well in low-pressure settings (Beilock and Carr, 2005). This means that capable students can seem to 'forget' what they know because anxiety has taken over their thinking. Sometimes test anxiety is a good thing; it boosts motivation, focus and effort, leading to higher grades. But we shouldn't underplay this issue for our reluctant and resistant students.

The hidden complexity of 'simple' errors

What we often call 'poor technique' may show unmet needs instead of student weaknesses. Here are some common issues found in examiner reports and what they might really mean:

- Copying errors might reflect visual processing difficulties, rushing due to anxiety or struggling to hold multiple pieces of information in working memory. These mistakes often come from feeling overwhelmed, not carelessness.

- Unclear handwriting might indicate problems with motor skills, slow processing speed or physical tension from anxiety that affects fine motor control. Writing can become much harder for students under pressure.

- Not reading questions carefully may come from language processing difficulties or anxiety. Missing obvious questions often shows that students feel overwhelmed, lack good question selection strategies or shut down when faced with dense text. They aren't lazy; they're trying to protect themselves from failing again.

By understanding these causes, we can create targeted interventions instead of offering one-size-fits-all advice that doesn't tackle the true challenges students face.

The exam technique audit

Before we offer solutions, we need to work out each student's specific technique challenges. Traditional methods usually give the same advice to all students, ignoring the unique patterns that affect their success or failure, but these questions will help students identify their personal technique patterns:

1. Do you often mix up numbers or copy things wrong when you're under pressure?
2. Is your working out clear enough for someone else to follow easily?
3. Are you answering the actual question or just the one you think it's asking?
4. Do you stop to check if your answer makes sense in real life?
5. Are you remembering to include units and format things properly?
6. Are you showing enough working to get method marks, even if the final answer is wrong?

Of course, how we present these self-check questions matters just as much as the questions themselves. Different students will need different approaches. For example, EAL students might benefit from seeing the questions with visual supports, and it's often helpful to pair them with peers who can support their understanding. Neurodivergent students may find a full checklist overwhelming, so focusing on just two or three questions at a time, with clear examples, can make a big difference.

For students with anxiety, framing the activity as a way to learn more about themselves (rather than as a test) reduces any pressure. Let them reflect privately, and share the theory behind exam stress so they know they're not alone. Dyslexic students might prefer audio versions or the chance to respond verbally, while students with dyscalculia often benefit from visual scaffolds like number lines and a focus on concepts over speed.

The real power of this audit isn't in the checklist, it's in what we do with the answers. When a student consistently makes copying errors, they need a different kind of support than someone who struggles with interpreting questions or managing time. Sometimes what looks like carelessness is actually working memory overload. Sometimes a pattern of mistakes reveals anxiety triggered by certain question types. Often students don't even realise these patterns exist until we help them spot them. That moment of recognition can be a turning point.

Strategic question selection

Once students start to recognise their own exam patterns, we can help them take more control over how they approach a paper. One of the simplest but most powerful shifts is moving away from the idea that you have to answer questions in order. For anxious students especially, that 'start at question one and work through' advice can backfire: if the first question triggers panic, it can derail the whole paper.

Instead, teach them to think strategically. GCSE Foundation Tier maths papers are designed to ease students in, with the first few questions typically pitched at Grades 1–3. They're meant to be accessible, but 'accessible' is personal. A percentage question might feel easy to one student and completely overwhelming to another.

Helping students understand the structure of the paper and giving them permission to choose where to start can be a game changer. It's not about shortcuts; it's about confidence and control.

> **Classroom activity: Traffic light question triage**
>
> Instead of working through an exam paper from start to finish, students learn to scan the whole paper first and sort the questions by confidence level:
>
> - **Green**: 'I can definitely do this.'
> - **Amber**: 'I think I can do this with a bit of effort.'
> - **Red**: 'This looks tricky – I'll come back to it.'
>
> Give students a past paper and a few minutes to colour-code each question using this system. Then, have them start with their green questions, move on to amber and leave red until last. Some students might prefer to cut up the paper and tackle each question individually, and a small minority even start at the back and work forwards, from the hardest to the easier questions; whatever helps them feel more in control.

This strategy helps students manage their anxiety by giving them choice and structure. It turns a daunting paper into something they can navigate with confidence.

The traffic light strategy works best when it's flexible. Different students will need different ways into it, and that's okay – this is about helping everyone feel more in control.

- For students with anxiety, start small. Use just the first ten questions to avoid overwhelm, and let them categorise privately at first. It's important they know that marking a question red doesn't mean they're failing – it just means they're being strategic.

- Students with ADHD often benefit from more physical engagement. Try using coloured stickers instead of written symbols, and build in movement breaks between sorting and solving. You can even turn it into a game: 'How fast can you spot your green questions?'
- For those with dyslexia, visual stress can be a real barrier. Offer coloured overlays, allow peer support for reading and keep the focus on the maths – not the language.
- Students with autism may prefer clear, consistent routines. Give them specific examples for each colour category, allow extra time to make decisions and stick to the same colour scheme every time.

The key idea here is that choice reduces anxiety. When students feel they have agency over how they tackle a paper, they're more likely to engage with it productively even when it's tough.

Formula sheet mastery: Making it work for them

The formula sheet in GCSE maths isn't just a list, it's a chance to give students a bit of breathing room. But unless they know how to use it well, it can end up being more of a distraction than a help. Here's a simple three-step routine to help students turn the sheet into something they actually *use,* not just glance at.

1. Fill the gaps (5 mins): Start with the stuff they always forget. Let them write reminders straight onto the sheet during practice In a sense, they are constructing their own knowledge organiser from the formula sheet:

    - prime and square numbers
    - angle facts (180° in a triangle, 360° around a point)
    - conversions they mix up (cm to m, minutes in an hour)
    - times tables they stumble on
    - vocabulary they confuse (mean, median, mode).

    This isn't cramming, it's about feeling more in control.

2. Add visuals (2 mins): Next, get them to sketch quick diagrams next to key formulas:

    - a trapezium by the area formula
    - a prism by the volume one

- circle parts labelled near circumference and area
- SOHCAHTOA written out with a triangle or however you have taught them.

These little cues can help jog memory when the pressure is on.

3. Pick your top three (1 min): Finally, have them circle or mark the three formulas they're most likely to need based on what they've struggled with or seen in recent papers. It's a quick way to cut down on panic and save time.

> **Classroom activity: Formula sheet drill**
>
> Give students a formula sheet and eight minutes to run through all three steps. Repeat this in mocks and low-stakes tests until it becomes second nature. The goal is fluency – not just with the maths, but with the tools that support it.

Just like with question triage, this routine can flex to suit different needs:

- **dyslexia:** Use colour coding, symbols and audio cues
- **ADHD:** Break it into short, timed chunks, add movement
- **autism:** Keep the order consistent, give clear examples
- **dyscalculia:** Focus on visuals and concrete examples
- **EAL:** Add notes in their first language, use universal symbols.

The formula sheet should feel like *theirs*. When students personalise it and practise using it, it stops being just a random page and starts being a tool they trust.

Breakfast maths

More and more schools are recognising that students need a proper warm up before stepping into high-stakes exams. Just like athletes wouldn't compete without stretching first, students with maths anxiety benefit from a gentle cognitive warm up that helps them settle and focus.

The best pre-exam sessions strike a balance: familiar enough to feel safe, but with just enough challenge to get brains ticking. The tone matters too: it should feel calm and supportive, not like a last-minute panic. Often, these sessions happen in the refectory, with a drink and a snack, which helps set a relaxed atmosphere.

Good breakfast maths activities:

- mix familiar procedures with light twists to keep things interesting
- offer solo, pair and group options so students can choose what suits them
- include a range of difficulty levels so everyone can find a way in
- connect clearly to exam content, but without feeling like cramming.

To make sure everyone can take part, consider offering flexible formats for students managing anxiety. Research shows that retrieval practice right before an exam can boost performance, but only if it feels supportive (Agarwal and Bain, 2019). If it feels like a test, it can backfire.

Not every student can make it to morning sessions. Transport issues, caring responsibilities or social anxiety can get in the way. That doesn't mean they should miss out. You can offer take-home versions that still give them a chance to warm up:

- short videos they can watch on the way in
- audio files for quick fact recall
- simple confidence-boosting exercises for exam morning
- breathing and relaxation techniques.

Supporting different learning needs with exam preparation

Preparing students for exams isn't just about teaching content. It's about making sure every learner has a fair chance to show what they know. That means recognising that standard approaches don't work for everyone, and that disadvantage comes in many forms: neurodivergence, language barriers, disrupted education, poverty, trauma or simply low confidence built up over years.

- Students with ADHD often struggle with focus and stamina in exams, but they may also be quick thinkers with strong pattern recognition. Breaking papers into short, timed sections, using movement breaks, and practising self-advocacy can help them manage their attention more effectively.

- Autistic students may find comfort in the structure of maths, but the unpredictability of exam settings can be unsettling. Clear routines, visual schedules and practice in the actual exam room can reduce anxiety and build confidence.

- Dyslexic students often have strong reasoning skills but may be held back by reading-heavy questions. Audio versions (where allowed), visual methods and extra time can help shift the focus back to their mathematical thinking.

- For students with dyscalculia, traditional exams can feel inaccessible. Visual supports, concrete materials and a focus on conceptual understanding – rather than speed or symbol manipulation – can open up new ways to succeed.

- EAL learners face the dual challenge of understanding the maths and the language it's wrapped in. Pre-teaching vocabulary, using glossaries, and reducing cultural assumptions in word problems can make a big difference.

- And then there are students whose challenges aren't always visible. They might be tired, hungry, anxious or juggling responsibilities outside school. For these learners, small adjustments (a calm environment, a predictable routine, a sense of belonging) can be just as powerful as formal accommodations.

Inclusive exam prep isn't about lowering expectations. It's about removing barriers so every student can walk into the exam room with a fair shot.

Rethinking feedback

Inclusive exam preparation isn't just about what happens before the test, it's also about how we respond afterwards. For many students, especially those who've experienced repeated failure, feedback feels like judgement. If we're not careful, marking can reinforce the idea that they're 'bad at maths', even when the truth is more nuanced. Dylan Wiliam reminds us that assessment is the bridge between teaching and learning. But for that bridge to hold, it has to feel safe (Wiliam, 2013).

Most schools have moved away from public ranking or seating students by grade. But subtler practices – returning papers in mark order, reading out scores, focusing only on mistakes – can still leave students feeling exposed. Instead, feedback should build confidence, not chip away at it. Try these approaches:

- **Double marking:** First, mark the paper as usual. Then go back and highlight marks lost to technique rather than misunderstanding – things like copying errors, missing units, or misreading the question. Present both scores. A student might see:

  - Actual score: 34/80 (Grade 2)
  - Understanding score: 48/80 (Grade 4)
  - Technique improvement potential: 14 marks.

This shifts the narrative. Instead of 'I'm bad at maths,' students see where small changes could make a big difference.

- **Non-graded feedback:** For some students, especially those near grade boundaries, removing the grade altogether can help. Use symbols like ✓ (method correct), ⚠ (technique issue), ? (unclear working) to guide reflection. Comments like 'Your algebra's solid – let's work on reading questions carefully' keep the focus on growth. You can even turn feedback into a challenge: 'There are five technique errors in the first 20 marks – can you find them?' This builds analytical skills without the sting of correction.

- **Marking to first mistake:** Another option is to record how far a student gets before their first technique error. Many start strong but lose focus as the paper goes on. Tracking this helps students see their potential and gives a clear, personal goal: 'Let's push that first mistake further next time.'

Managing emotional responses to assessment

Even the most thoughtful marking strategies can fall flat if students are already feeling defeated. That's why how we *talk* about assessment matters just as much as how we mark it.

When students respond emotionally to feedback, our role isn't to dismiss those feelings or rush to reassure. It's to validate their experience and gently redirect their focus toward what's *changeable*.

Script box: When confidence drops after mocks

When someone says, 'I got Grade 2 again. I'm never going to pass.'

- Say: 'Grade 2 is actually a pass – you've already passed, just not at Grade 4 yet. Let's look at where those marks came from. I can see three types of errors here – which one feels most fixable?'
- Not: 'Don't worry, you'll do better next time.'
- Follow-up: 'Your mathematical thinking is stronger than this grade suggests. Which type of error do you want to tackle first?'

Script box: When time pressure feels overwhelming

When a student says: 'I always run out of time.'

- Say: 'That usually means we're spending too long on questions we're unsure about. Let's practise choosing questions more strategically.'
- Not: 'You need to work faster.'
- Follow-up: 'Let's time you doing questions you're confident with – I bet you're quicker than you think.'

These kinds of responses help students feel heard, while gently shifting the focus from personal inadequacy to practical strategies.

From page-turners to problem solvers

Awarding bodies sometimes refer to 'page-turners': students who skip over long, text-heavy exam questions. Faced with four- or five-mark problems wrapped in unfamiliar contexts and dense language, many choose to move on, not because they can't do the maths but because they don't know where to start. This kind of avoidance is often more about language processing than mathematical ability. With the right support, most students can access these higher-value questions and even come to feel confident tackling them.

One of the most effective strategies is to model how to break down the problem visually. Drawing diagrams, underlining key information, and mapping out what's being asked helps students turn a wall of text into something they can work with. These aren't just scaffolds for students who struggle with reading, they're good practice for everyone. As Amjad Ali points out in *SEND in the Classroom*, if a strategy helps one student, it may well help them all (Ali, 2023). He uses the analogy of a building entrance: why have steps and a ramp when everyone could just use the ramp? The same principle applies here. Visual modelling and structured approaches to problem solving build confidence and resilience across the board.

Using examiner reports constructively

Feedback from teachers is important for building student confidence, just as feedback from examiners can improve our teaching methods. We should view examiner reports as helpful tools for reflection, not as reasons to assign blame. When reports point out common student mistakes, we can reframe our questions from 'Why do they always get this wrong?' to 'What factors might be causing these problems?' This shift encourages a more supportive environment for improvement.

Often, the issue isn't the maths concepts themselves, but comes from how the questions are worded or from cultural references that some students may not understand. Students might also use valid methods that the marking scheme does not recognise, or they might face accessibility challenges that we didn't consider. By looking at examiner reports with empathy and analysis, we can learn valuable information. This helps us identify trends, improve our teaching strategies, and support fairer assessment practices.

The spoof analysis technique

One way to help students reflect on their exam technique without triggering defensiveness is to take the pressure off entirely by using fictional work. The spoof analysis approach involves creating sample responses that contain common technique errors but still show sound mathematical thinking. Students then act as examiners, identifying what went wrong and suggesting improvements.

Start by collecting typical mistakes from anonymised student work: things like copying errors, misreading the question or giving the wrong final answer despite correct working. Then, write fictional examples that mirror these issues without resembling any real student. The key is realism without personalisation.

In class, ask students to analyse the spoof paper: What does this student understand? What technique issues cost them marks? How could they improve? Once they've practised spotting errors in someone else's work, they're often more able to reflect on their own. It's a gentle way to build self-awareness and exam literacy without shame.

Embedding exam resilience across the year

Effective exam technique doesn't come from a last-minute push. It builds gradually, through consistent routines and low-stakes practice. A year-long approach helps students develop habits that support both confidence and performance.

In the autumn term, focus on foundations: introduce assessment language, build familiarity with exam formats and establish feedback routines that feel safe. As winter sets in, shift towards technique (use mock exams as learning tools, not just tests, and help students spot their own patterns). Spring is the time for intensive practice: rehearse strategies, manage anxiety and adapt support for individual needs. By summer, the focus should be on maintaining confidence, calming routines, final prep and emotional support.

Even ten minutes per lesson spent on one aspect of exam technique can make a big difference, an intrinsic part of the 5Rs approach. Embedding these strategies into regular teaching helps students see exam skills as part of their mathematical learning, not something separate or scary.

> **Hear from the expert: Graham Cumming, former Pearson Maths Subject Specialist**
>
> 'Here's my advice for students facing an exam paper:
>
> - Read each question slowly, more than once if you need to; make sure you have a plan of approach before you start working. Everything in the question is there to help you; all the information given will be needed somewhere in your solution. (There are one or two exceptions to this, of course, like train timetable questions [in] which you have to choose the appropriate information.)
> - Even if you think you can't finish the question, you should be able to score the first mark; make that your aim and you never know, the subsequent marks might follow.
> - Always show all your working; it helps the examiner follow your thinking and might help you too.
> - The first five questions are designed to put you at ease and should be ones you can answer; but don't rush them and lose marks through haste.
> - If a reason is asked for and carries one mark, a sentence will do; it doesn't need more than that.'

When teachers feel anxious too

Supporting students through exam season can be emotionally demanding, especially when we're carrying our own worries about outcomes, expectations or simply doing right by our class. After all, we're not just managing content; we're managing emotions, both theirs and ours.

It's easy to feel unprepared when faced with a student in distress and you might avoid talking about the exam altogether, focus only on the maths, or feel overwhelmed by the pressure to 'fix' their anxiety. Sometimes, we even take their panic personally, as if it reflects on us. But recognising our own emotional responses is the first step in supporting students effectively.

A calm, grounded reply makes all the difference. When a student says, 'I'm never going to pass,' you don't need to rush in with reassurance. Instead, acknowledge the feeling: 'I can see this feels overwhelming – that makes sense given what you've been through.' You can normalise it: 'Most people feel nervous before exams. It means you care.' And then redirect: 'Let's focus on one small thing you can control right now.'

Sometimes, the best support is knowing when to step back. If a student's anxiety feels beyond what you can manage, it's okay to refer to a counsellor, mental health lead or specialist service. Your role isn't to eliminate anxiety altogether. It's to model calmness, offer practical strategies and help students feel less alone in the process.

Adapting to your setting

- **GCSE classrooms:** Start early. From Year 10, include exam techniques in regular lessons. Use monthly mini-mocks to help students focus on how they approach questions, not just on their answers. Celebrate improvements in techniques, like better question selection and clearer calculations, just like you celebrate progress in math content.
- **Resit students:** Address emotional barriers first. Many feel embarrassed or frustrated from past attempts, so acknowledge this before teaching new techniques. Emphasise new strategies instead of repeating unsuccessful ones. Let them know that they are not failing; they just need to find the right approach.
- **Vocational support contexts and adult education:** Make it relevant. Connect exam skills to workplace habits, such as accuracy, time management and problem solving. Use real-world examples in practice questions and show how exam strategies relate to professional demands. Adults may appreciate clear links between exam techniques and job skills.
- **One-to-one intervention:** Focus on building confidence. Allow students to pick which topics to work on, and tackle one technique at a time. Keep sessions calm, focused and at the learner's pace.
- **SEND:** Adapt strategies to meet students' individual needs. What works for others may need changes. Collaborate with SEND coordinators, support staff and families to tailor your approach and ensure consistency.
- **EAL:** Bilingual resources and peer support can help a lot. Connect new techniques to methods they used in their home countries. Use cultural references to support understanding, not just translation.

Key research points

- Beilock and Carr: *Working Memory and Stress* (2025)
  - Key takeaway: This study showed that performance drops significantly under exam pressure, especially for students with limited working memory or additional processing needs. Many students underperform not because they don't understand the content, but because stress interferes with their ability to access it.

- Use it: Help students recognise stress responses early. Practise exam strategies in low-pressure settings first, then gradually increase the challenge to build resilience.

- Ramirez and Beilock (2011): *Anxiety and Low-Stakes Practice*
  - Key takeaway: Research found that low-stakes practice reduces test anxiety more effectively than extra revision. Students often feel they need more content, when what they really need is more confidence.
  - Use it: Prioritise regular, low-pressure exam practice over last-minute cramming. Create safe spaces where students can rehearse technique without fear of failure.

- Educational Psychology Research: *Strategic Question Selection*
  - Key takeaway: Studies show that students who choose which questions to answer first perform better than those who work through papers sequentially. Strategic thinking improves performance and reduces anxiety, especially for students who freeze on unfamiliar questions.
  - Use it: Teach question triage strategies early. Practise scanning papers and choosing starting points in mock exams and classroom activities.

- Cummins: *Cultural and Linguistic Contexts* (2000)
  - Key takeaway: Cummins highlighted how students from different educational backgrounds may struggle with unfamiliar exam formats and language. Misunderstanding exam expectations can mask mathematical ability, especially for EAL learners or those from non-UK systems.
  - Use it: Provide explicit instruction in UK exam conventions. Validate alternative methods and use bilingual or culturally relevant resources where possible.

Reflection questions

- How do I currently approach assessment, and how could I adapt it to better support resistant or anxious learners? Do my current methods build confidence or reinforce fear? Are there small shifts I could make to reduce pressure while still promoting progress?
- Can I identify students whose mathematical understanding seems stronger than their results suggest? What patterns can I see in their work – are marks being lost to avoidable errors?
- How confident do I feel supporting students with exam anxiety or emotional barriers? Would extra training, peer support, or collaboration with pastoral staff help me feel more prepared?
- What recurring technique errors do I see when marking? Could they be addressed through targeted teaching? How can I build these into my planning?

- How might my own experiences of assessment shape how I respond to struggling students? Do my own school experiences help or hinder my empathy? Are there assumptions I might need to challenge?
- What support networks do I have access to for students with high anxiety or additional needs? Who should I refer to – SENDCos, mental health leads, counsellors? What relationships could I build to strengthen my support system?

Next steps

1 Review current practices: Look over recent mock exams to find common mistakes among different student groups. Are students losing marks due to avoidable errors? Are some students not doing well even if they have good math skills?
2 Try one new strategy: Pick a technique from this chapter that will help your most struggling learners. This could be about choosing questions, using formula sheets, or analysing answers. Start with something manageable.
3 Start small: Introduce one exam technique, like question triage, to a single class. Keep it low-pressure and incorporate it into regular lessons.
4 Create inclusive resources: Change exam prep materials to help EAL learners, students with different learning needs, and those who feel anxious. Use images, simpler language, and varied formats.
5 Build support networks: Connect with SENDCos, EAL experts, and mental health staff. Good relationships help when supporting students with complex needs. Learn from Amjad Ali: *SEND in the classroom*.
6 Ask for student feedback: Talk to students about what they find difficult about exams and which strategies work for them. Their feedback can guide your approach and reveal hidden challenges.
7 Integrate techniques throughout the year: Don't wait until the last term to prepare for exams. Include exam skills in everyday teaching so they become habits.
8 Create a supportive assessment environment: Use feedback and grading methods that build confidence. Avoid practices that could shame or discourage students, especially those with bad experiences.
9 Work with colleagues: Share successful strategies and learn from each other. A team approach to exam prep helps improve outcomes for all students.

Chapter 12
Re-vision: Seeing Maths Differently

From revision resistance to mathematical resilience

Sarah stares at her revision timetable: 'Two hours of maths every evening.' It felt hopeful when she wrote it. Now, facing her third GCSE resit, it feels like punishment. She's tried revision before, many times, and it's never worked. Why would this time be different?

Sarah's story is familiar. For resistant learners – resitters or Year 10/11 students – traditional revision often repeats the very methods that failed them. Reading revision guides they didn't understand. Practising procedures that never made sense. Cramming facts that won't stick.

This chapter transforms revision from a source of stress into a pathway for mathematical resilience. We explore the concept of 're-vision' – literally seeing mathematics again, but differently. Through inclusive, trauma-informed approaches, we help students like Sarah rediscover maths without shame or fear.

The best time to start revising? Now. Even 30 minutes a day can make a huge difference. The challenge is helping students find where that half-hour fits into their routine.

Why students resist revision

The transformation begins with understanding that resistance isn't laziness, it's protection. Students who refuse to revise are often protecting themselves from re-experiencing shame, embarrassment, confusion and failure. Some simply can't be bothered because they don't value the success of it, as we have seen from Chapter 1. Our task is to create revision experiences so positive, so different from what came before, that students are willing to risk engaging again.

> **Student voice: The emotional reality of revision**
>
> Before we explore techniques, we need to hear what students actually experience when we mention revision:
>
> - 'I don't know where to start – there's too much to learn and I'm rubbish at all of it.'
> - 'Every time I try to revise, I just remember failing before. Why would this time be different?'
> - 'I can't concentrate for long enough to revise properly. My mind just wanders.'
> - 'Reading revision guides makes me feel stupid. The words get jumbled up.'

These voices reveal layers of complexity that standard revision advice ignores. When we tell students to 'make a revision timetable' or 'read through your notes', we're often asking them to engage with the very activities that have previously caused them distress.

The problem with traditional revision

Most revision guidance assumes students have a basically positive relationship with learning and just need better techniques. For resistant learners, this assumption is fundamentally flawed. Traditional approaches fail because they don't address the emotional barriers that prevent engagement.

Consider the typical revision advice: create a quiet study space, make a timetable, use past papers, practice regularly. For a student with processing difficulties, quiet spaces might feel isolating. Many students will never have access to quiet spaces because of domestic situations. For someone with ADHD, rigid timetables can feel suffocating. For students carrying mathematical trauma, being faced with a full past paper triggers anxiety rather than building confidence. These techniques are not inherently bad, but they weren't designed for students who struggle. We need approaches that work specifically for reluctant, anxious and resistant learners.

Research from Helen Howell and Ross Morrison McGill, in *The Revision Revolution*, says that the process of revision should start the moment that something is learned, not left until weeks before an exam (Howell and Morrison McGill, 2022). Their advice is to build mini-revision moments into every lesson through retrieval practice and spaced repetition.

When students refuse to revise

Let's address the infuriating question: what do you do when students simply won't engage with revision at all? When they don't turn up to revision sessions, refuse to take materials home or sit in class with arms folded declaring 'I'm not doing this.' That's if they are there at all. Avoidance can manifest in non-attendance. We see swathes of revision sessions set up in settings across the country as the exams approach, and attendance is a key determinant on their usefulness and success. It's often a lot of wasted effort and expense.

This complete refusal isn't defiance. It's often the final stage of learned helplessness. Students who've experienced repeated failure in mathematics develop sophisticated avoidance strategies. From their perspective, refusing to try makes perfect sense: if you don't engage, you can't fail again.

Understanding the protection mechanism

Complete refusal typically stems from one of several sources. Some students carry deep shame and embarrassment from previous experiences: 'I revised for six weeks last time and still got Grade 2 so what's the point?' Others feel overwhelmed by the gap between where they are and where they need to be: 'I'm so far behind, I'll never catch up.' Many are protecting themselves from re-experiencing trauma: 'If I don't try, I can't be humiliated again.'

For students with ALN, refusal often masks frustration with inaccessible methods. Traditional revision approaches may literally not work for how they process information, leading to the reasonable conclusion that 'revision doesn't work for me.'

Disguising revision

One of the most effective approaches for completely resistant students is to remove the word 'revision' entirely. Instead, we create opportunities for mathematical engagement that don't feel like formal study.

Asking students to create content works remarkably well. 'Could you make a TikTok video explaining percentages?' feels completely different from 'revise percentages for homework'. Students who refuse traditional revision often engage enthusiastically with creating posters, writing instructions or recording explanations, or testing new apps 'to see if they're any good'.

Choice and control

When students feel powerless, returning some control can unlock engagement. This means offering choices at every level: what to work on, how to work on it, when to stop, where to work and who to work with.

For students experiencing trauma responses, choice is essential. The ability to say 'I'm done' and actually stop without consequences can be the difference between engagement and shutdown. Start with tiny commitments: 'Would you be willing to look at this for two minutes?' Most will agree to do something that small, and often, once they're engaged, natural curiosity takes over. If you're clever, you can put a timer on the work and leave it running for as long as the student is engaged: quite often two minutes easily becomes five minutes, developing more confidence once you point this out. There are some lovely apps which support focus as well as a project management tool called the Pomodoro.

Classroom activity: The Pomodoro technique

The Pomodoro technique is used to help people focus on the task at hand (Gupta, 2025). It encourages working in short bursts with regular breaks to increase overall productivity. In my experience, using a range of different timers works well and introduces a fun element. You could use an online timer, but that detracts from the engaging physical timer to focus on.

Ask students to undertake a revision exercise, answer questions or listen to a YouTube clip for 10 minutes – the duration of the first timer you set. Everything else is put aside and out of view apart from the exercise and the timer. When the buzzer goes off, time is up and they stop for a short break. Repeat the Pomodoro for a series of short maths bursts.

Teaching tip: Meeting students where they are

Evidence from the US shows that one in five 13–17 year-olds are almost permanently on YouTube (Faverio and Sidoti, 2024), with Tik Tok and Instagram widely used too. Ofcom have recently released figures on UK YouTube usage, showing 16–35 year-olds driving the YouTube streaming trend (Ofcom, 2025). If you can't beat them, join them! Encourage students to approach revision differently from traditional methods by making use of this trend. Ask them, 'What are the best YouTube maths channels? What about TikTok?' and help to co-create a recommendation list.

Classroom dialogue: Working with complete refusal

This conversation shows how to approach a student who's completely shut down:

Teacher: 'I notice you haven't been coming to revision sessions.'
Student: 'What's the point? I'm going to fail anyway.'
Teacher: 'It sounds like you're protecting yourself from disappointment. That makes complete sense after what you've been through.'
Student: 'Exactly. I'm done with maths.'
Teacher: 'I hear you. What if we didn't call it revision? What if we just hung out and looked at some maths problems together – no pressure, you can leave anytime?'
Student: 'I suppose... but I'm not promising anything.'
Teacher: 'Perfect. No promises needed. Just show up if you feel like it.'

Notice how the teacher validates the student's feelings rather than trying to convince them they're wrong. The offer is completely low-stakes, with multiple escape routes built in. This approach often works where direct persuasion fails.

Building from strength: The foundation of effective revision

Once we've established that students are willing to engage (even minimally), we need to build from what they *can* do rather than focusing on what they can't. This strength-based approach is crucial for resistant learners who've had their deficits highlighted repeatedly.

Every student has some mathematical knowledge, even if it's not immediately obvious. The challenge is finding it and using it as a foundation for growth. This might be practical skills like handling money, pattern recognition from gaming or spatial awareness from sports. Start there, celebrate it, then gradually connect it to curriculum content.

The traffic light assessment

One of the most powerful tools for building from strength is the traffic light assessment using revision cards. Rather than overwhelming students with everything they need to know, this approach makes learning visible and manageable. For students on the cusp of Grade 3 into Grade 4, this revision will be enough to take them over the line.

1. Lay revision cards across several tables and give students a task: sort them into three piles. Green cards represent topics they definitely know, amber cards are things they sort of know and red cards are complete unknowns. (If using as a group exercise, give students a list to use.)
2. The magic happens in what we do next. Instead of focusing on the red cards (the deficit approach most students expect), start with green. Say, 'Let's make your green cards even stronger. Practice until you cannot get them wrong.' This builds confidence and creates positive momentum.
3. Next, tackle amber cards – moving them to green through targeted practice. When students have built substantial confidence you can gradually introduce red card topics, one at a time. This prevents overwhelm while maintaining the success-building momentum.

For students with different learning needs, this approach adapts naturally:

Learning Need	Adaptation
Dyscalculia	Use physical cards rather than lists; provide visual examples.
Anxiety	Allow private sorting initially; start with fewer cards.
Autism	Provide clear criteria for each category; use consistent colours.
Dyslexia	Include visual representations; offer peer support for reading.
EAL	Provide bilingual cards where possible; use peer translation.

This systematic approach addresses the most common barrier to effective revision: not knowing where to start. By making all content visible and categorised, students can make informed choices about their learning priorities.

The 5Rs framework: Trauma-informed revision

The 5Rs curriculum emerged to help students who have previously struggled with the subject. Instead of a one-size-fits-all approach, this framework provides a different path to success for resistant learners. It's a valuable tool for revision, as it provides a clear, structured progression that can be tailored to individual students' needs. Tell students why each of the 5Rs is pertinent.

The 5Rs framework: A week-by-week implementation plan

Weeks 1–2: 'Recall' Start with a diagnostic assessment to identify students' existing knowledge. In the first week, do daily 5-minute fact practice using flashcards, apps or games. In the second week, introduce **spaced repetition**, mixing facts from Week 1 with new content. The goal is for students to retrieve basic and fundamental facts quickly and without hesitation.

Weeks 3-5: 'Routine' In Week 3, introduce a daily routine, such as the 'Corbettmaths 5-a-day,' starting at a level below what you think is appropriate to build confidence. In Week 4, allow students to choose their preferred routine (e.g., time of day or location), and in Week 5, establish peer accountability partnerships. The aim is for students to complete this routine independently every day from this point onward.

Weeks 6-9: 'Revise' Using a traffic light assessment, start by revising 'green' topics (already mastered) in Week 6 to build momentum. In Week 7, work on 'amber' topics (some understanding) using different methods. In Week 8, tackle one 'red' topic (little to no understanding) with a completely new approach. Finally, in Week 9, connect the revised content to real-world applications. The objective is for students to be able to explain the concepts using their preferred revision methods.

Weeks 10-11: 'Repeat' In Week 10, have students practice exam questions in a supportive environment, allowing for open books and peer help. In Week 11, gradually decrease support to simulate exam conditions. By the end of this period, students should be attempting exam questions with **confidence**, not panic.

Week 12: 'Readiness' This final phase focuses on exam technique and anxiety management. Provide time for students to develop motor skills for using mathematical tools like calculators. The ultimate goal is for students to feel prepared and equipped with coping strategies for any difficulties they might encounter.

In subsequent terms each lesson can contain all five elements, if time allows.

Recall and routine: Building secure foundations

Traditional approaches often assume students remember basic facts when they don't. The 'recall' element systematically addresses fundamental knowledge gaps without shame, embarrassment or judgement. For students with dyscalculia, this might mean visual-spatial fact storage rather than rote memorisation. For students with ADHD, it could involve movement-based practice and gamification.

The key insight is that gaps in fundamental knowledge are simply missing building blocks that can be systematically addressed. When students realise they can actually learn and remember the facts, their whole relationship with maths shifts. Usually, they simply haven't been asked to recall this fundamental information often enough over time.

'Routine' maths develops confidence through familiar patterns and regular practice. For anxious students, routine provides security. For students with executive function difficulties, it removes the daily decision-making burden about what to practice.

One of the most successful routines is Corbettmaths 5-a-day, which provides five questions daily at appropriate levels. What makes this work for resistant learners is its consistency: the same format and expectations with gradual progression, so students know exactly what to expect, reducing anxiety while building fluency.

> **Hear from the expert: Jonny Hall, Mathsbot.com**
>
> 'When you achieve fluency with a mathematical idea, it's like moving from painstakingly sounding out each word to effortlessly reading a book. The operations and processes become automatic, almost second nature – freeing your brain to work on the next brick in the wall.'

> **Teaching tip: Making daily maths sustainable**
>
> When introducing daily maths habits, start small. Even five questions might feel overwhelming. Start with just one question per day for the first week, then gradually build up.

Revise: Fresh approaches to familiar content

The 'revise' element is where 're-vision' becomes literal. Students encounter familiar content through completely different methods – visual approaches for those who struggled with abstract symbols, practical applications for those who couldn't see relevance, collaborative work for those who felt isolated in their confusion. Encourage students to find YouTube clips, or use TikTok, and follow people for GCSE maths content. A caveat to this is that these items are not quality controlled, so discussion should take place around which are the best channels. Hannah Kettle (see Further Reading and Resources), for example, runs live exam paper walk-throughs which are supremely popular with GCSE maths students of all ages.

Revision is where alternative methods and models also become crucial. A student who struggled with the column method for multiplication might discover they can multiply successfully using the grid method or Vedic techniques (see Chapter 6). The content remains the same, but the pathway to understanding is different.

Repeat: Building confidence through success

'Repeat' involves practising what they have just revised, with exam-style questions, but in a supportive, low-stakes environment. Students work with question types they'll encounter in assessments, but with scaffolding, peer support and multiple attempts allowed.

This element addresses one of the biggest fears resistant learners face: unexpected question formats in exams. By familiarising students with assessment language and expectations gradually, we reduce anxiety while building genuine exam confidence.

Readiness: Exam technique and emotional preparation

'Readiness' encompasses both practical exam skills and emotional preparation for assessment. This includes everything from reading questions carefully to managing anxiety on exam day.

For many resistant learners, poor exam technique rather than mathematical misunderstanding causes failure. Addressing technique separately from content allows students to gain marks they've actually earned, often making the difference between grades.

Confronting 'I'm too stupid' beliefs: Cognitive restructuring for mathematics

One of the most damaging beliefs resistant students carry is the conviction that they're intellectually incapable of mathematical thinking. This isn't just low confidence, it's a deeply held identity that affects every learning interaction (see Chapter 1).

Classroom dialogue: Challenging 'stupid' beliefs

Here's how to respond when students express these beliefs:

Student: 'I'm just too stupid to understand this. My brain doesn't work for maths.'
Teacher: 'I hear you saying that you feel stupid, but I see someone who's found the best method for them. There's a big difference.'

Notice how the teacher validates the feeling without accepting the belief and reframes struggle as mismatch rather than deficiency.

Throwing out curriculum order

Traditional mathematics education follows a carefully sequenced curriculum, but resistant learners may benefit from completely different sequences based on interest, relevance or accessibility.

A student fascinated by music might begin with frequency ratios and sound waves, naturally encountering fractions, decimals and graphs. Someone interested in social justice might start with statistical analysis of inequality, developing data handling and percentage skills. The key insight is that mathematical concepts connect in multiple ways. We don't have to follow traditional pathways if they haven't worked for particular students.

> **Classroom activity: Understanding revision**
>
> Explore the meaning of 'revision' early on with learners by asking them what it means to them. Use a carousel activity to ask the following questions:
>
> - What can you revise?
> - When can you revise?
> - How can you revise?
> - Who could you revise with?
> - Where can you revise?
>
> Unpick the responses, highlighting suggestions such as working on YouTube, buddying up with a friend or working through revision card sets or revision guides regularly. Some of the best revision guides for mathematics are the new *Ready, Set, Go* series from Kangaroo Maths and Mel Muldowney (see Further Reading and Resources). Ask what else students can do to help themselves, then probe further: 'What else? Is there anything else?'

The journey from resistance to resilience is through small, consistent actions. For students who've experienced mathematical trauma, long, intensive study sessions often recreate the conditions that caused them to disengage in the first place. Instead, we need to offer revision experiences that feel manageable and sustainable. This approach also acknowledges the reality of their lives – often busy, complex and filled with competing demands.

1. **Eliminating barriers:** Before asking students when they'll revise, we need to identify what stops them from engaging with mathematics. These barriers might be practical (no quiet space at home), emotional (anxiety triggered by mathematical content) or cognitive (working memory difficulties that make traditional study methods ineffective). Common barriers include:

    - 'I always forget' → Need external reminders and cues.
    - 'I don't have time' → Need micro-habits that fit existing routines.

- 'I don't know what to do' → Need pre-planned, specific activities.
- 'It makes me anxious' → Need emotional support and gradual exposure.

Once we understand specific barriers, we can design habits that work around them rather than requiring students to overcome them through willpower alone.

2. **Micro-habits that work:** Sustainable revision starts small. Instead of asking for 30 minutes, ask for 30 seconds. One question, not five. This isn't lowering expectations – it's smart design. Small wins build confidence and momentum, while unrealistic goals often lead to giving up. Linking revision to existing habits – like checking a maths problem after scrolling your phone or before watching Netflix – makes it easier to stick with. These micro-habits feel natural because they're built into routines students already follow.

3. **Sustainable growth:** Once micro-habits are firmly in place, we can gently build on them – gradually increasing commitment over time. This might take weeks or even months, and that's absolutely fine. The aim isn't short-term intensity, but a lasting, healthy relationship with maths. Different learners will need different pacing, e.g. those with ADHD may thrive on variety and stimulation. Autistic students and adult learners often prefer predictable routines; many like working steadily through a revision guide. Learners with anxiety may need flexibility, especially during stressful periods. Students with processing difficulties may simply need more time to consolidate before moving forward.

> **Hear from the expert: Mel Muldowney, Just Maths**
>
> 'The best way to revise maths is to 'do maths'... Don't just practice topics you can already do but mix it up with things that you know you need to work on.'

Supporting diverse learners

Revision works best when it's flexible, accessible and designed with difference in mind. Some students need structure and predictability; others thrive on variety and movement. The key is offering choices and removing barriers from the start. Helpful strategies include:

- short, focused sessions with regular breaks
- visual methods and hands-on tools to make abstract ideas concrete
- audio versions or minimal-text resources to reduce reading load

- predictable routines with clear expectations
- flexibility to reduce pressure during stressful periods
- movement, creativity and collaboration to sustain engagement
- extra time and scaffolding to support processing and memory
- linking revision to personal interests or everyday contexts
- encouraging independence for those who prefer working solo
- celebrating progress visibly to build motivation and confidence.

When revision is designed to meet real needs across the spectrum, it's more inclusive, more effective and more empowering.

Alternative approaches when traditional methods fail

Sometimes, despite our best efforts to adapt traditional revision methods, students remain completely disengaged. In these situations, we need fundamentally different approaches that barely resemble conventional revision but still develop mathematical understanding.

Project-based revision

Long-term projects that require mathematical skills can engage learners who find traditional revision meaningless. These projects need to be genuinely interesting and produce real outcomes that matter. Examples might include:

- planning and budgeting a charity fundraising event
- designing and testing improved home or work equipment
- analysing and presenting research on issues students care about
- creating business plans for student enterprises.

The maths comes from genuine need, making engagement more likely even for highly resistant learners. This approach is great in vocational settings.

Revision through creation

When students resist consuming revision content, engaging them in creating mathematical content can be transformative. This approach works because it shifts the power dynamic – students become experts sharing knowledge rather than struggling learners consuming it. Creating TikTok videos explaining mathematical concepts appeals to many young people's existing interests while requiring deep understanding to explain concepts clearly. Students who refuse to read revision guides might enthusiastically script, film and edit short videos about percentages or graph interpretation.

Real-world application

Disguising revision as practical problem solving removes the emotional baggage associated with formal study. Students who refuse mathematical revision might willingly engage with personal budgeting, home improvement calculations or analysing gaming statistics. This approach works because it connects abstract mathematical concepts to concrete purposes. The key is choosing contexts that genuinely matter to students.

Revision through movement and social interaction

For students with attention difficulties, traditional desk-based revision can feel like torture. Alternative approaches that incorporate movement and social interaction often succeed where static methods fail. Encourage them to work in a different way – on whiteboards around the room or to use glass writing pens on the windows.

Mathematical walks around the school or local area can reinforce geometric concepts, estimation skills and real-world applications. Board games and card games such as Top Trumps develop strategic thinking and number fluency. Physical manipulatives and hands-on activities make abstract concepts concrete.

Peer tutoring serves a similar function. Sometimes students engage when asked to help other learners, finding confidence in their relative expertise. The social element is crucial for many resistant learners who've felt isolated in their mathematical struggles. Working collaboratively removes the embarrassment of individual failure while providing peer support and alternative explanations.

Assessment and progress: Measuring what matters

Traditional progress measures often miss the gains that matter most for resistant learners. A student who moves from complete refusal to willingness to attempt one problem has made enormous progress, even if their mathematical skills haven't visibly improved.

Inclusive assessment recognises multiple types of progress:

- **Academic progress**: Grade improvements, topic mastery, increased accuracy.
- **Emotional progress**: Reduced anxiety, increased willingness to attempt, improved mathematical identity.
- **Behavioural progress**: Better attendance, sustained effort, help-seeking behaviour.
- **Social progress**: Collaboration with peers, supporting others, asking questions.

For many resistant learners, emotional and behavioural progress precedes academic gains. Students need to feel safe and capable before they can access mathematical learning effectively.

Celebrating success

Recognition needs to match students' values and communication preferences. Some students thrive on public acknowledgement, while others prefer private feedback. Some value tangible rewards, while others find intrinsic satisfaction in progress itself.

The key is observing what genuinely motivates each student rather than assuming universal preferences. A quiet word of encouragement might mean more to an anxious student than a certificate, while public recognition might devastate someone who prefers to remain invisible.

Technology: Tools that transform access

Thoughtfully chosen technology can remove barriers that prevent students from engaging with revision. The most effective educational technology for resistant learners provides immediate feedback, allows multiple attempts without penalty and adapts to individual learning pace.

Any digital tools should accommodate different ways of accessing information: adjustable text size and contrast for visual difficulties, screen reader compatibility for blind and partially sighted users, keyboard navigation for motor difficulties or multiple input methods (touch, voice, keyboard). The goal is ensuring that technology reduces rather than creates barriers.

Beyond the exam

For resistant learners, revision isn't just about passing GCSE maths. It's about rebuilding confidence and developing a healthier relationship with learning. When students learn to persist through difficulty, they gain skills that transfer far beyond the classroom.

The strategies in this chapter work because they support the whole learner. They build resilience, self-belief and the ability to keep going even when things feel hard. That's what revision is really about. So, start small. Try one disguised revision activity, adapt one method for a student who needs it, or have one honest conversation about past maths experiences.

Adapting to your setting

- **GCSE classrooms:** Revision starts from day one. Talk about revision – how, when, where, what works. Employ every strategic approach suggested here. Match the student to the revision that works for them.
- **Resit students:** Encourage reluctant revisors to find what works for them, whenever they can do it and for however long. It starts on day one. Their starting point isn't that they know nothing.
- **Vocational support contexts and adult learners:** Make revision relevant and show the connection between revising for maths as well as revising for every other part of their course. Adult learners often prefer a more traditional book/worksheet based approach.
- **One-to-one intervention:** Focus on building confidence, one question, one topic at a time. Find self-assessment exercises such as those on mathsbot.com, transum.org and onmaths.com which demonstrate tangible and immediate success. Keep sessions calm, focused and at the learner's pace.
- **SEND:** Adapt strategies to meet students' individual needs. What works for others may need changes. Collaborate with others involved to tailor revision.
- **EAL:** Bilingual resources and peer support can help a lot. Use rich, collaborative revision tasks and allow weaker English language students to be supported by stronger ones, who can support the language comprehension while they both support each other's maths.

Key research points

- Howell and Morrison McGill: *The Revision Revolution: How to build a culture of effective study in your school*[1]

- Key takeaway: That revision starts the moment that anything is learned. That students need to be taught how to revise and that this will have ramifications for every part of the curriculum, not just the maths.
- Use it: Read, digest and implement the suggestions
- The Mathematical Association: 5Rs curriculum (see Further Reading and Resources)
  - Key takeaway: Reluctant, resistant maths learning should benefit from the 5Rs curriculum approach following key routines which tackle all of the major issues espoused in this book
  - Use it: Implement the 5Rs approach and garner feedback on impact from students who may appreciate the consistency in the approach. See key reasons why this tackles exam success for them.

Reflection questions

- How do I currently define 'revision' and how might that definition need to shift?
- Which strategies in this chapter could help me re-engage students who've previously shut down?
- Have I ever mistaken resistance for laziness? What might be driving a student's refusal to revise?
- What changes could I make to help students feel safer and more in control during revision?
- How can I use students' strengths – rather than their gaps – as starting points for revision?
- Which students might benefit from disguised or alternative revision approaches?
- What role does emotional safety play in how I plan and deliver revision activities?
- Am I offering enough choice, flexibility and low-stakes entry points to revision?
- What support do I need to feel confident adapting revision for different learning needs?

Next steps

1 Try disguised revision with a student who refuses traditional approaches.
2 Implement the traffic light assessment to help overwhelmed students prioritise.
3 Adapt one technique for a student with specific learning needs.
4 Start micro-habits with students who struggle to maintain revision routines.

Conclusion: Changing the Narrative

This book is here to walk alongside you: not to add pressure, but to offer practical tools for the real challenges you face. It's about helping students move from resistance to resilience, one revision moment at a time. Whether you're in a classroom, a college or a learning hub, this toolkit is designed to work in the settings we actually find ourselves in.

And let's be honest: those settings are tough right now. Teacher shortages are no longer background noise, they're front and centre. In 2024/25, secondary recruitment met just 62 per cent of the Department for Education's target (Department for Education, 2025). The National Foundation for Educational Research (NFER) reports that secondary initial teacher training in 2023/24 reached only half of its goal, and vacancy rates remain high. Retention is also a growing concern. Nearly one in five teachers now say they're considering leaving the profession, with workload and wellbeing cited as key reasons (McLean et al., 2024).

At the same time, the pressures on students are increasing. According to NHS England, one in five children and young people aged 8 to 25 now show signs of a probable mental health disorder, including anxiety and depression (NHS, 2023). Many are still dealing with the emotional fallout of the pandemic, and it shows up in the classroom – often as resistance, withdrawal or behaviour that masks deeper needs.

No student comes to school to be difficult. There's always a reason behind the behaviour. Hopefully, this book has helped you feel more equipped to respond – not just with strategies, but with understanding.

And here's the impact of that understanding. The most recent GCSE maths data shows:

- 831,556 entries across all ages
- 58.2 per cent of all entries achieved Grade 4 or higher

- 71.9 per cent of 16 year-olds reached Grade 4 or above
- 17.1 per cent of 17+ resit students achieved Grade 4 or higher – that's 35,351 young people (Joint Council for Qualifications, 2024; FFT Education Datalab, 2024)..

That last number matters. It's the size of a packed football stadium. And for every one of those students, it's a door opened to further study, better job prospects and more choices.

So when students push back, when they say 'I'm not doing this' or 'I'll never pass', you now have the tools and the facts to respond. Share the stories. Celebrate the wins. Help them see what's possible. Give me a borderline Grade 3/4 student any day. That's where the challenge is real – and the reward is even greater.

References

Chapter 1

Chinn, S. (2019) *Mathematics Anxiety in Secondary Students in England*. Available at: www.stevechinn.co.uk/articles/maths-anxiety (Accessed: 9 October 2025).

Kowsun, J. (2004) 'This innumerate isle', *TES Magazine*, September. Available at: www.tes.com/magazine/archive/innumerate-isle (Accessed: 10 July 2025).

Maths Anxiety Trust (2018) *Official Figures*. Available at: https://mathsanxietytrust.com/official-figures.html (Accessed: 14 July 2025).

National Numeracy (n.d.) *What is Maths Anxiety & What Causes It?*. Available at: www.nationalnumeracy.org.uk/what-issue/about-maths-anxiety (Accessed: 10 July 2025).

Parker, C. (2015) *Cultivating a growth mindset in mathematics*. Available at: https://ed.stanford.edu/news/cultivating-growth-mindset-math (Accessed: 9 October 2025).

Pearson (n.d.) *A Guide to Tackling Maths Anxiety: Building more confident and resilient learners, teachers and communities*. Available at: www.pearson.com/uk/content/dam/one-dot-com/one-dot-com/uk/documents/subjects/mathematics/guide-to-tackling-maths-anxiety-power-maths-report.pdf (Accessed: 14 July 2025).

Swan, M. (2005) *Improving learning in mathematics: challenges and strategies*. Available at: www.stem.org.uk/resources/library/resource/26057/1 (Accessed: 9 October 2025).

Swan, M. (2006) 'Learning GCSE mathematics through discussion: what are the effects on students?', *Journal of Further and Higher Education*, 30(2), pp. 229–241.

Chapter 2

Al-Tamimi, H.A.H. and Kadiyala, N.R. (2025) 'Relationship between numeracy skills and financial literacy: A review', *The Economics Journal*. Available at: www.theeconomicsjournal.com/article/view/464/8-1-23 (Accessed: 14 July 2025).

BBC (2023) 'Bradford student passes maths GCSE after 13 years and four attempts'. Available at: www.bbc.co.uk/news/uk-england-leeds-66609459 (Accessed: 9 October 2025).

Beilock, S.L. and Maloney, E.A., 2015. Math anxiety: A factor in math achievement not to be ignored. *Policy Insights from the Behavioral and Brain Sciences*, 2(1), pp. 4–12.

Chinn, S. (2012) *The Trouble with Maths: A Practical Guide to Helping Learners with Numeracy Difficulties*. 2nd edn. London: Routledge.

Chinn, S. (2019) *Mathematics Anxiety in Secondary Students in England*. Available at: www.stevechinn.co.uk/articles/maths-anxiety (Accessed: 9 October 2025).

Department for Education (2023) *Curriculum and Assessment Review: Final Report*. London: Department for Education. Available at: https://www.gov.uk/government/publications/curriculum-and-assessment-review-final-report (Accessed: 18 November 2025).

Department for Education (2024) *Interim curriculum review: GCSE resit rules need 'greater nuance'*. London: Department for Education.

Department for Education (2024) *Key Stage 4 and 16–18 Performance Tables*. London: Department for Education. Available at: https://www.gov.uk/government/statistics/key-stage-4-and-16-to-18-performance-tables (Accessed: 18 November 2025).

Department for Education (2024) *Survey of Adult Skills 2023: national report for England*. Available at: www.gov.uk/government/publications/survey-of-adult-skills-2023-national-report-for-england (Accessed: 9 October 2025).

Dowker, A., Sarkar, A. and Looi, C.Y., 2016. Mathematics anxiety: What have we learned and what do we still need to know? *Frontiers in Psychology*, 7, p. 508.

Education Policy Institute (2023) *Post-16 Education and Disadvantage Report*. London: EPI. Available at: https://epi.org.uk/publications-and-research/post-16-education-and-disadvantage (Accessed: 18 November 2025).

Gigerenzer, G. (2014) 'Risk literacy: The mother of all numeracy skills', *Risk Management*, 16(2), pp. 16–19.

Gov.uk (2013) 'New GCSE Grades Research Amongst Employers'. Available at: https://assets.publishing.service.gov.uk/media/5a7f1655e5274a2e8ab4a08a/2013-11-01-bmg-research-with-employers-on-new-gcse-grades.pdf.

Gov.uk (2025) *Key Stage 2 attainment and lifetime earnings*. Available at: https://assets.publishing.service.gov.uk/media/6867d497fe1a249e937cbcdb/Key_Stage_2_attainment_and_lifetime_earnings_reseach_report_-_July_25.pdf (Accessed: 14 July 2025).

Lusardi, A. and Mitchell, O.S. (2014) 'The economic importance of financial literacy: Theory and evidence', *Journal of Economic Literature*, 52(1), pp. 5–44.

National Foundation for Educational Research (2024) *OECD (PIAAC) Survey: England's Youth Skills Show Dramatic Improvement Since 2012*. Available at: www.fenews.co.uk/skills/oecd-piaac-survey-englands-youth-skills-show-dramatic-improvement-since-2012

National Numeracy (2017) *Essentials of Numeracy*. Available at: www.nationalnumeracy.org.uk/what-numeracy/essentials-numeracy (Accessed: 14 July 2025).

National Numeracy (2018) *Measuring Mathematical Resilience: An application of the construct of resilience to the study of mathematics (2012)*. Available at: www.nationalnumeracy.org.uk/research-and-resources/measuring-mathematical-resilience-application-construct-resilience-study (Accessed: 9 October 2025).

National Numeracy (2018) *Numeracy and managing your Health*. Available at: www.nationalnumeracy.org.uk/research-and-resources/numeracy-and-managing-your-health (Accessed: 14 July 2025).

National Numeracy (2024) *Parents pass fear of maths on to their children, new Mumsnet research suggests*. Available at: www.nationalnumeracy.org.uk/news/parents-pass-fear-maths-their-children-new-mumsnet-research-suggests (Accessed: 14 July 2025).

Office for National Statistics (ONS) (2024) *Young people not in education, employment or training (NEET), UK*. Available at: www.ons.gov.uk/employmentandlabourmarket/peoplenotinwork/unemployment/bulletins/youngpeoplenotineducationemploymentortrainingneet/august2024

Open University Business School (2019) 'Lack of confidence with numbers preventing parents from helping children with maths homework'. Available at: www.open.ac.uk/business-school/news/lack-confidence-numbers-preventing-parents-helping-children-maths-homework.

Robey, C. and Jones, E. (2015) *Engaging Learners in GCSE Maths and English*. Available at: https://learningandwork.org.uk/wp-content/uploads/2020/04/Engaging-Learners-in-GCSE-Maths-and-English.pdf (Accessed: 9 October 2025).

Sherrington, T. (2019) *Revisiting Dylan Wiliam's Five Brilliant Formative Assessment Strategies*. Available at: https://teacherhead.com/2019/01/10/revisiting-dylan-wiliams-five-brilliant-formative-assessment-strategies/ (Accessed: 9 October 2025).

TES (2019) 'Tes people of the year: Lauren Reid'. Available at: www.tes.com/magazine/archive/tes-people-year-lauren-reid (Accessed: 9 October 2025).

Wiliam, D. (2009) *Embedded Formative Assessment*. Bloomington, IN: Solution Tree Press.

Wuttke, M. (2014) 'Statistical literacy for journalism students', *Journal of Journalism Education*, 69(1), pp. 62–73.

Chapter 3

ariamark (2013) *The day I passed maths*. Available at: www.youtube.com/watch?v=Ls9Cg8iaq1s (Accessed: 9 October 2025).

Bell, E. (2020) *CfEM blog: the 'Focused 15' at Grimsby Institute - The ETF*. Available at https://etfoundation.co.uk/news-and-events/news-and-updates/etf-blogs/cfem-blog-the-focused-15-at-grimsby-institute-the-etf/ (Accessed: 9 October 2025).

Busby, E. (2024) *School leaders condemn 'remorseless treadmill' of GCSE English and maths resits*. Available at: www.tes.com/magazine/analysis/secondary/gcse-resits-everything-you-need-know (Accessed: 9 October 2025).

Daily Mail (2022) *Oldest ever GCSE maths student passes his exams AGED 92*. Available at: www.dailymail.co.uk/news/article-11144809/Oldest-GCSE-maths-student-passes-exams-AGED-92-Ex-RAF-engineer-gets-highest-possible-grades.html (Accessed: 9 October 2025).

Dweck, C. (2016) *Mindset: The new psychology of success*. New York: Ballantine Books.

Education Policy Institute (2025) *English and Maths Resits: Drivers of Success*. Available at: https://epi.org.uk/publications-and-research/english-and-maths-resits-drivers-of-success/ (Accessed: 9 October 2025).

Joint Council for Qualifications (2024) *Provisional English and Mathematics GCSE Results - June 2024 (England Only - aged 17)*. Available at: www.jcq.org.uk/wp-content/uploads/2024/08/Post-16-England-GCSE-English-and-Maths-summer-2024.pdf (Accessed: 9 October 2025).

Leicester College (2020) *How further education transformed my life*. Available at: https://leicestercollege.ac.uk/news/darren-hankey-case-study (Accessed: 9 July 2025).

Pekrun, R. (2025) *Has the 'cogsci revolution' forgotten about emotion?*. Available at: www.tes.com/magazine/teaching-learning/general/has-cogsci-revolution-forgotten-about-emotion (Accessed: 9 October 2025).

Robey, C. and Jones, E. (2015) *Engaging Learners in GCSE Maths and English*. Available at: https://learningandwork.org.uk/wp-content/uploads/2020/04/Engaging-Learners-in-GCSE-Maths-and-English.pdf (Accessed: 9 October 2025).

Royal Society (n.d.) *Survey with teachers on the impact of COVID-19 on mathematics education*. Available at: https://royalsociety.org/news-resources/projects/mathematics-education/royal-society-acme-maths-education-and-covid-19/ (Accessed: 9 October 2025).

Steward, S. and Nardi, E. (2002) 'I could be the best mathematician in the world if I actually enjoyed it: Part 1', *Mathematics Teaching*, (179), June. Available at: http://nrich.maths.org/content/id/15183/ElenaNardiSusanStewardATM-MT179-41-44.pdf (Accessed: 9 July 2025).

Tes reporter (2025) 'GCSE resits: a guide to retaking maths, English and other exams', *Tes*, 17 June. Available at: www.tes.com/magazine/analysis/secondary/gcse-resits-everything-you-need-know (Accessed: 14 July 2025).

Wiliam, D. (2009) *Assessment for learning: why, what and how?* London: Institute of Education, University of London.

Chapter 4

AQA (n.d.) *All About Maths: GCSE Mathematics*. Available at: www.aqa.org.uk/all-about-maths/spec-8300#teaching-resources (Accessed: 9 October 2025).

Foster, C. (2019) 'The fundamental problem with teaching problem solving'. Available at: https://atm.org.uk/write/MediaUploads/Journals/MT265/MT26503.pdf (Accessed: 4 September 2025).

Mccrea, P. (2020) *Extract: Motivated Teaching by Peps Mccrea*. Available at: www.ambition.org.uk/blog/extract-motivated-teaching-peps-mccrea/ (Accessed: 9 October 2025).

Sherwood, J. (2018) *How To Enhance Your Mathematics Subject Knowledge: Number and Algebra for Secondary Teachers*. Oxford: Oxford University Press.

US Department of Education (2008) *The Final Report of the National Mathematics Advisory Panel*. Available at: https://files.eric.ed.gov/fulltext/ED500486.pdf (Accessed: 9 October 2025).

Williams, D. (2017) *The importance of cognitive load theory (CLT)*. Available at: https://set.et-foundation.co.uk/resources/the-importance-of-cognitive-load-theory (Accessed: 9 October 2025).

Chapter 5

Burns, N. (2021) 'Metacognitive Modelling – Where Does it Fit in the Classroom?' Available at: https://educationblog.oup.com/secondary/science/metacognitive-modelling-where-does-it-fit-in-the-classroom (Accessed: 9 October 2025).

Chinn, S. (2012) *The Trouble with Maths: A Practical Guide to Helping Learners with Numeracy Difficulties*. London: Routledge.

Chinn, S. (2020) *How to Teach Maths: Understanding Learners' Needs*. London: Routledge.

Young, C. (n.d.) 'Knowledge Organisers'. Available at: https://colleenyoung.org/lesson-planning/knowledge-organisers/ (Accessed: 9 October 2025).

Chapter 6

Chinn, S. (2019) 'Conceptual Learning – an example using times tables'. Available at: www.stevechinn.co.uk/articles/conceptual-learning-an-example-using-times-tables (Accessed: 9 October 2025).

Chinn, S. (2019c) 'Dyscalculia'. Available at: www.stevechinn.co.uk/dyscalculia/what-is-dyscalculia (Accessed: 9 October 2025).

Hattie, J. (2009) *Visible Learning: A Synthesis of Over 800 Meta-Analyses Relating to Achievement*. Abingdon: Routledge.

Morgan, J. (2019) *A Compendium Of Mathematical Methods: A handbook for school teachers*. London: Hachette Learning.

National Numeracy (2019a) *A Guide to Tackling Maths Anxiety*. Available at: www.pearson.com/content/dam/one-dot-com/one-dot-com/uk/documents/subjects/mathematics/guide-to-tackling-maths-anxiety-power-maths-report.pdf (Accessed: 8 September 2025).

Patall, E.A., Cooper, H. and Robinson, J.C. (2008) 'The effects of choice on intrinsic motivation and related outcomes: A meta-analysis of research findings', *Psychological Bulletin*, 134(2), pp. 270–300.

The Education Hub (2019) 'An introduction to cognitive load theory'. Available at: https://theeducationhub.org.nz/wp-content/uploads/2021/03/An-introduction-to-cognitive-load-theory-v2.pdf (Accessed: 9 October 2025).

Chapter 7

Casey, H., Cara, O., Eldred, J., Grief, S., Hodge, R., Ivanič, R., Jupp, T., Lopez, D. and McNeil, B. (2006) *You wouldn't expect a maths teacher to teach plastering....* Available at: https://dera.ioe.ac.uk/id/eprint/22311/2/doc_3550.pdf (Accessed: 9 October 2025).

Dickinson, P. and Hough, S. (2012) *Using Realistic Mathematics Education in UK classrooms*. Centre for Mathematics Education, Manchester Metropolitan University.

English and Maths Booth (2021) *Don't embed maths, enhance your maths! With Julia Smith*. Available at: www.fenews.co.uk/podcast/em-booth-enhance-your-maths/ (Accessed: 9 October 2025).

LA Times (1999) *Mars Probe Lost Due to Simple Math Error*. Available at: www.latimes.com/archives/la-xpm-1999-oct-01-mn-17288-story.html (Accessed: 9 October 2025).

National Numeracy (2019) *Gateway to Growth: what employers need from education and skills*. Available at: www.nationalnumeracy.org.uk/research-and-resources/gateway-growth-what-employers-need-education-and-skills (Accessed: 9 October 2025).

Robey, C. and Jones, E. (2015) *Engaging Learners in GCSE Maths and English*. Available at: https://learningandwork.org.uk/wp-content/uploads/2020/04/Engaging-Learners-in-GCSE-Maths-and-English.pdf (Accessed: 9 October 2025).

Tech Startups (2020) *How a simple math error of putting a decimal point in the wrong place resulted in a 7-year delay of Spain's S-80 submarine and a $2.67 billion in cost overruns*. Available at: https://techstartups.com/2020/12/11/here-is-how-a-simple-math-error-of-putting-a-decimal-point-in-the-wrong-place-led-to-7-year-delay-of-spains-s-80-submarine-and-2-67-billion-in-cost-overruns/ (Accessed: 9 October 2025).

Zarnadze, B. (2023) *Mathematics in context: Do Ratio Tables help students make sense of maths problems?* Available at: www.et-foundation.co.uk/wp-content/uploads/2023/02/Do-ratio-tables-help-FE-maths-learners-make-sense-of-realistic-maths-problems_Harlow-College-CfEM-action-research-report-2021-22.pdf (Accessed: 9 October 2025).

Chapter 8

GeoGebra (no date) *GeoGebra*. Available at: www.geogebra.be (Accessed: 1 December 2025).

Mathematical Association (no date) *Mathematical Association*. Available at: https://m-a.org.uk/ (Accessed: 1 December 2025).

Swain, J. and Swan, M. (2007) *Eight Principles for Effective Teaching*. Available at: https://ccpathways.co.uk/wp-content/uploads/2016/06/Eight-Principles-for-effective-teaching.pdf (Accessed: 10 October 2025).

Chapter 9

Barton, C. (2025) 'Just give them a calculator'. Available at: https://eedi.substack.com/p/just-give-them-a-calculator (Accessed: 9 October 2025).

Francome, T. (2016) 'Empty protractor'. Available at: https://atm.org.uk/write/MediaUploads/Journals/MT253/MT253-16-11.pdf (Accessed: 9 October 2025).

gravylookout (2007) 'World Freehand Circle Drawing Champion'. Available at: www.youtube.com/watch?v=eAhfZUZiwSE (Accessed: 9 October 2025).

Chapter 10

Chinn, S.J. and Ashcroft, R.E. (2017) *Mathematics for Dyslexics and Dyscalculics*. 4th edn. Chichester: Wiley.

Dweck, C. (2016) *Mindset: The new psychology of success*. New York: Ballantine Books.

Education Endowment Foundation (2018) 'Metacognition and Self-regulated Learning: Guidance Report'. London: Education Endowment Foundation.

Foster, C. (2019) 'The fundamental problem with teaching problem solving'. Available at: https://atm.org.uk/write/MediaUploads/Journals/MT265/MT26503.pdf (Accessed: 4 September 2025).

Mattock, P. (2019) *Visible Maths*. Carmarthen: Crown House Publishing.

Polya, G. (1945) *How to Solve It: A New Aspect of Mathematical Method*. Princeton, NJ: Princeton University Press.

Pritchard, B. (2022) 'Working with worked examples – Simple techniques to enhance their effectiveness'. Available at: https://educationendowmentfoundation.org.uk/news/eef-blog-working-with-worked-examples-simple-techniques-to-enhance-their-effectiveness (Accessed: 9 October 2025).

Chapter 11

Agarwal, P.K. and Bain, P.M. (2019) *Powerful Teaching: Unleash the Science of Learning*. San Francisco: Jossey-Bass.

Ali, A. (2023) *SEND in the Classroom: Maximising the Learning of Students with Special Educational Needs*. Suffolk: John Catt Educational Ltd.

Beilock, S.L. and Carr, T.H. (2005) 'When high-powered people fail: Working memory and "choking under pressure" in math', *Psychological Science*, 16(2), pp. 101–105.

Cummins, J. (2000) *Language, Power and Pedagogy: Bilingual Children in the Crossfire*. Clevedon: Multilingual Matters.

Wiliam, D. (2013) 'Assessment: The Bridge between Teaching and Learning', *Voices from the Middle*, 21(2), pp. 15–20.

Chapter 12

Faverio, M. and Sidoti, O. (2024) *Teens, Social Media and Technology 2024*. Available at: www.pewresearch.org/internet/2024/12/12/teens-social-media-and-technology-2024/ (Accessed: 9 October 2025).

Gupta, S. (2025) *Why the Pomodoro Technique Is the Productivity Booster You Need to Try*. Available at: www.verywellmind.com/pomodoro-technique-history-steps-benefits-and-drawbacks-6892111 (Accessed: 9 October 2025).

Howell, H. and Morrison McGill, R. (2022) *The Revision Revolution: How to build a culture of effective study in your school.* John Catt Educational Ltd.

Ofcom (2025) *Tuning into YouTube: UK's media habits revealed*. Available at: www.ofcom.org.uk/media-use-and-attitudes/media-habits-adults/tuning-into-youtube-uks-media-habits-revealed (Accessed: 9 October 2025).

Chapter 13

Department for Education (2025) *Teacher workforce: secondary and further education.* Available at: www.nao.org.uk/wp-content/uploads/2025/04/teacher-workforce-secondary-and-further-education-summary.pdf (Accessed: 9 October 2025).

FFT Education Datalab (2024) *GCSE results 2024: The main trends in grades and entries.* Available at: https://ffteducationdatalab.org.uk (Accessed: 12 September 2025).

Joint Council for Qualifications (JCQ) (2024) *GCSE (Full Course) outcomes by age, all specifications at key grades, England, Northern Ireland & Wales, Results Summer 2024.* Available at: www.jcq.org.uk (Accessed: 12 September 2025).

McLean, D., Worth, J. and Smith, A. (2024) *Teacher Labour Market in England Annual Report 2024.* Available at: www.nfer.ac.uk/publications/teacher-labour-market-in-england-annual-report-2024/ (Accessed: 9 October 2025).

NHS (2023) *One in five children and young people had a probable mental disorder in 2023.* Available at: www.england.nhs.uk/2023/11/one-in-five-children-and-young-people-had-a-probable-mental-disorder-in-2023/ (Accessed: 9 October 2025).

Further Reading and Resources

Access Maths Pentagon Problem: www.accessmaths.co.uk/uploads/4/4/2/3/44232537/pentagon_problem_1_-_functional_surface_area.pdf
AQA's Small Things Make a Big Difference – A guide to common errors in GCSE Mathematics: https://store.aqa.org.uk/content/gcse-maths-papers/AQA-SMALL-THINGS-BIG-DIFFERENCE.PDF
Artful Maths: www.artfulmaths.com/
Bouncy Balls: https://bouncyballs.org/
Churchill Fellowships – Educational travel funding opportunities to observe international vocational mathematics approaches: www.churchillfellowship.org/become-a-fellow/our-current-programmes/
Craig Barton's Podcast – listen to the episode with yours truly on the 5Rs curriculum approach (suitable for Year 11 and resitting students): https://mrbartonmaths.com/blog/
Corbettmaths: https://corbettmaths.com/
Eedi Newsletter – Craig Barton's weekly EEDI free newsletters are very informative and thought provoking: https://eedi.substack.com/about
Frayer Models: www.frayer-model.co.uk/
GeoGebra: www.geogebra.be/
Hannah Kettle: www.hannahkettlemaths.co.uk/
Kangaroo Maths Revision Guides: https://justaroo.co.uk/
Mathematical Association: https://m-a.org.uk/
Mathematical Hooks Padlet: https://padlet.com/tessmaths1/mathematical-hooks-bq5soikjnp05
The Maths Anxiety Trust: https://mathsanxietytrust.com/
Mathsbot Fluent Calculations: https://mathsbot.com/starters/fluentCalcs
Maths Careers: www.mathscareers.org.uk/
Maths Careers Posters: www.stem.org.uk/resources/library/collection/450137/maths-career-posters
MathShed: www.mathshed.com/en-gb/
MEI Contextualisation Toolkit: https://mei.org.uk/resource/9ae5796b-cf76-4ee1-ac9b-08d967d68474/
Ofqual's Guide to Coping with Exam Pressure: www.gov.uk/government/publications/coping-with-exam-pressure-a-guide-for-students
Onmaths – For exam practice: www.onmaths.com/
PixiMaths: www.piximaths.co.uk/
Realistic Mathematics Education: https://rme.org.uk/
Resourceaholic: www.resourceaholic.com/
TES 30-second Challenges: www.tes.com/teaching-resource/30-second-mental-maths-puzzle-11701413
Tom Scott, You Can't do Simple Maths Under Pressure: www.tomscott.com/usvsth3m/maths
Transum Games: www.transum.org/Software/Maths_Map

Index

Access Maths Pentagon Problem 68
adult learning/learners vi, 45, 56, 90, 113, 155, 169, 183, 187
algebra 43–5, 52, 118, 154
Ali, Amjad, SEND in the Classroom 166
alternative learning methods 74–5, 83, 184–5
anxiety, maths 4–5, 31, 49, 74–5, 90–1, 113, 131, 157–9
AQA Basic Skills Questions 57, 111
assessment 26, 53, 88–9, 109, 123, 142, 153, 156, 159, 164–7, 177–9, 185–6
autism, students with 4, 31, 38, 51, 61, 161–2

Barton, Craig 35, 138, 143
Beilock, S.L. 158, 169–70
Bell, Emma 35–6
Burns, Nathan 69

calculators 138–40, 143
Carr, T.H. 158, 169
Chinn, Steve viii, 12, 14, 23, 27, 61, 71, 78, 91, 149
classroom activities 7–11, 21–2, 24, 36–7, 46–7, 50–1, 68, 102, 110–11, 117–18, 135–6, 150, 160, 162, 176, 182
cognitive load theory 57, 76, 91
confidence building 5, 12, 26, 43, 45, 49, 59–60, 62–3, 67, 69–70, 75–8, 124–5, 130–1, 139, 147, 157–8
construction, maths in 54, 96, 100, 137–8
Corbett, John 65
Corbettmaths 5-a-day 65, 67, 179
Covid-19 pandemic 35, 130
cross-curricular approaches 95, 101, 106, 118–20, 124

Cumming, Graham 168
Cummins, J. 170
curriculum 19, 30, 32, 35–6, 39, 44, 59, 62, 105, 118–20, 154, 188

Department for Education (DfE) 19, 189
dialogues, classroom 5, 63, 70, 78, 87, 131–2, 152, 177, 181
Dickinson, P. 113
disengagement 31–3
diverse learners 37–8, 50–1, 85–6, 183–4
division methods 81–3
Dweck, Carol 34, 155
dyscalculia, students with 4, 13, 23, 51, 61, 76, 164, 179
dyslexia, students with 38, 85, 159, 161, 164

Ebbinghaus Forgetting Curve 67, 71
Education Policy Institute (EPI) 30, 39
English as additional language (EAL) vii, 4, 7, 85, 152, 159, 164, 169, 187
error analysis 53, 66, 134, 158–9
etymology 61–2, 67
exams 35, 88–9, 109, 130, 138, 157–70, 181

FFT Education Datalab 30
5Rs curriculum 35–6, 39, 49, 74, 167, 178–80, 188
fixed mindset 6, 34
fluency, mathematical 15, 35, 37–8, 43–57, 59
Focused 15 curriculum 35–6, 39
formative assessment 123
formula sheets 161–2
Foster, Colin 45, 148, 155
Francome, Tom 133
Frayer Models 69, 142
Functional Skills 90, 109–11, 113

games 37, 50, 134–6, 185
GCSE maths 19, 30, 32, 88–9, 109, 130, 138, 160–1, 180, 189–90
   classrooms 14, 26, 39, 56, 70, 88–90, 112, 126, 142, 155, 169, 187
   Foundation Tier 19, 39, 60, 160
   Higher Tier 60, 138
GeoGebra 121, 126, 132
geometry 100, 118, 129–30, 133, 137–8
Grandi, Clarissa 137
growth mindset 33–4, 37, 153

Hall, Jonny 37, 65, 180
Hankey, Darren 32, 34
Hattie, John 85, 91
health and fitness, maths in 21, 96, 100
hooks, mathematical 115–27
Hough, S. 113
Howell, Helen 174, 187

Jones, E. 27, 31, 95, 113

knowledge gaps 60, 68–9, 71, 88, 161, 179
knowledge organisers 68–9, 71, 88, 161

language barriers 151–2

Mathematical Association 126, 188
mathematical thinking 117, 120, 122
Mathsbot 37–8, 55, 65
Mattock, Pete 116, 150
Mccrea, Peps 55
McGill, Ross Morrison 174, 187
method choice 74–5, 84–9
mindsets 6, 33–4, 37, 153
mixed-method classrooms 87–8
Morgan, Jo 89–90
motivation 29–39
Muldowney, Mel 183
multiplication methods 46–7, 50, 73, 75–8

Napier's bones/lattice method 77
National Foundation for Educational Research 189
National Numeracy 4, 24, 26, 74, 95

National Research and Development Council 97, 113
neurodivergent students 4, 77, 159
Not in Education, Employment or Training (NEET) 19

one-to-one interventions 14, 26, 39, 56, 70, 90, 112, 126, 142, 154, 169, 187

partial products method 76–7
pattern recognition 49, 53, 116, 119
Pekrun, Reinhard 31
percentage questions 43–4, 52, 160
Polya, George 148, 155
post-16 learning 4, 56, 107
post-COVID pandemic 35
problem solving vii, 22, 26, 29, 43, 45, 147–56
project-based learning (PBL) 95, 108–9, 184
protractors 133, 135

Realistic Maths Education (RME) 95, 107–8, 113
real-world applications 21, 53–4, 95–6, 110, 185
Reid, Lauren 20
relevance, maths 23, 25, 71, 100, 109, 118, 121
resistance, mathematical vi, 3–15, 31–2, 43, 73, 173
resit students 14, 26, 29–30, 39, 56, 70, 90, 112, 126, 142, 155, 169, 187
revision methods vii, 173–88
RHINO (Really Here In Name Only) 33
Robey, C. 27, 31, 95, 113
Royal Society 35
rulers 132

self-directed study 37–8
Sherwood, Jemma 43, 47
social media 121, 176, 180, 185
Southall, Ed 116
spaced repetition 67, 178
special educational needs (SEND) vii, 4, 7, 13, 37, 56, 126, 169, 187

special educational needs coordinator (SENCo) 5, 106
statistics and probability 18, 118, 154
subtraction methods 79–81
Swan, Malcolm viii, 5, 12, 14, 126
sustainable teaching 32, 106

Target Number 50, 83
technology 21, 25, 54, 116, 121, 186
T Levels 105
tools, mathematical 129–43
traditional learning methods 4, 13, 30, 37, 48, 73–4, 77, 136, 159, 174–5, 179, 182, 184
traffic light assessment 36, 177–9

Transum Maths 37–8, 136–7, 142
trauma-informed revision 178–80

Vedic method 73, 77–8, 180
visualiser tool 121, 126, 132, 141
vocabulary, maths 62–4, 69, 152
vocational contexts 14, 26, 39, 56, 70, 90, 95–113, 126, 142, 155, 169, 184, 187

Ward, Jess 20
Wassan, Paul 54, 103
Whiston, Nicola 69
whole-school approaches 106
Wiliam, Dylan viii, 24, 27, 34, 57, 164
work-based learning 105

Other titles from Bloomsbury